J.P. Morgan

The Life and Deals of America's Banker

J.P. Morgan

The Life and Deals of America's Banker

Insight and Analysis into the Founder of Modern Finance and the American Banking System

JR MacGregor

JP Morgan – The Life and Deals of America's Banker

Copyright © 2019 JR MacGregor

All rights reserved. No portion of this book may be reproduced, stored in a retrieval system, or transmitted in any form or by any means – electronic, mechanical, photocopy, recording, scanning, or other – except for brief quotations in critical reviews or articles, without prior written permission of the publisher.

Published by CAC Publishing LLC.

ISBN 978-1-950010-29-5 paperback

ISBN 978-1-950010-28-8 eBook

Contents

Introduction 7

Chapter 1 Background 13

Chapter 2 Early Life 27

Chapter 3 Shortcomings 38

Chapter 4 Early Deals 45

Chapter 5 The Peabody Effect 52

Chapter 6 Jack Morgan 86

Chapter 7 High Finance & Low Times 94

Chapter 8 Turning Tides 115

Chapter 9 The Panama Canal 120

Chapter 10 Humble Pie 125

Chapter 11 Crash of 1907 129

Chapter 12 The Rise of Morgan 154

Chapter 13 The Sun Sets 187

Conclusion 216

Introduction

John Pierpont Morgan Sr., also known as J.P. Morgan, revolutionized the financial world. He brought America and by extension the entire world into the twenty-first century by infusing the trade and banking industries with his ideas.

He was responsible for creating many structured and organized entities as trusts, one of the largest banks in the world, the largest steel production company in America, and one of the largest railroads in the country.

Along the way, he endured a lot of pain and hardship but overcame it by focusing on his work, which was his elixir.

On a personal level, Morgan was highly complex in his behavior, oscillating from total confidence to retiring within himself to absolute diffidence and self-effacement. His confidence was marked with silence, and his diffidence was marked with bravado.

Add to this his expensive upbringing and it becomes difficult to really peg this towering man of vision and intellect.

Morgan's father was his initial role model and guide in navigating the world of international business. Morgan himself was astute, with a unique understanding of money. It was almost a visceral appreciation of how money worked and how it could be harnessed to leverage other resources. Money to him was like a natural resource that could be harnessed and utilized.

At the turn of the nineteenth century, America had begun to transition from an agrarian society and a colonist's mind-set to an industrialized country with a nation-state mind-set. With that change in social activity and aggregate mind-set came the need to have a higher derivative of monetary and fiscal policy and all the tools commensurate with that elevation. In other words, the world of banking needed to change, which included public as well as private finance.

The once simple and geometric relationship between trade and finance had changed. What was just a simple relationship between saver and lender was now inadequate. What was now required had not yet been contemplated. This new world of high finance was only obvious to such men as George Peabody, Marcus Goldman, and Junius Pierpont Morgan.

New instruments were developed to finance endeavors. New structures were created, and many of these came about by men who blurred the lines between public and private finance.

J.P. Morgan ascended through the business world with great difficulty but with a powerful imagination, constantly combating anti-monopoly politicians and presidents who were opposed to large business.

Among the robber barons and titans of the period, J.P. Morgan stood at the center. If it were not for J.P. Morgan, Andrew Carnegie, as successful as he was, would not have been able to sell Carnegie Steel for $480 million, making him a very wealthy man.

J.P. Morgan was a man of exceptional character. He was determined, aggressive, and ambitious and stopped at nothing to get what he wanted.

As smart and sharp as he was, however, Morgan created his banking empire only during the last thirteen years of his life. His early years were spent trying, making mistakes, and developing his abilities. In his lifetime, he worked with two different presidents to avert market failures. He was able to stop the bleeding in the financial markets when they crashed. Twice.

He was also the man behind the Panama Canal. Just as important as the physical structure that cut its way from the Pacific Ocean to the Atlantic, the financial structure was equally important in being able to pay for the materials, equipment, and labor. It was Morgan who structured it and raised the money for it.

He died with a net worth of less than $30 billion, adjusted for inflation today, but he controlled more than 100 billion. If he saw fit to buy something, he could raise an almost unheard amount of money.

By wielding such vast sums of money, he amassed a tremendous amount of power and influence in the last fifteen years of his life.

But his life was not easy. Even though he could sail the Hudson in his private yacht or buy any piece of art that his heart desired, the degree of personal and public stress he endured was immeasurable. Some attribute this stress to smoking as many as twenty cigars a day.

Even though his life was stressful, he enjoyed collecting art and sailing. He was a man of great accomplishment and commensurate success, which hid the peak insecurities and accompanying anxiety

He was afflicted with many health issues and physical problems, which made him unhappy, insecure, and sensitive. In spite of his anxieties and weaknesses, though, he created one of the largest banking houses in the world only to be broken down by the then trust-busting U.S. government.

Chapter 1 Background

John Pierpont Morgan Senior's great-great-great-great grandfather was Miles Morgan, a man from the seventeenth century. He had traveled from Wales to Massachusetts Bay in 1626. That was the first time a Morgan stepped onto the shores of the New World.

Pierpont's paternal grandfather, Joseph Morgan III, was the man who reorganized the Hartford Fire Insurance Company to form the Aetna (Fire) Insurance Company.

Pierpont's maternal grandfather was John Pierpont, a minister and poet. He was eventually removed from his place because of his radical views, and he was also an abolitionist.

Pierpont's maternal uncle, James Lord Pierpont, was a cofounder of Yale University and a songwriter whose most famous composition is "Jingle Bells." The song had originally been published as "The One-Horse Open Sleigh" in 1857.

Those are impressive accomplishments to be concentrated in two houses—the Morgans and the Pierponts.

J.P. Morgan was born to Junius Spencer Morgan and Juliet Pierpont April 17, 1837, in Hartford, Connecticut.

During his lifetime, J.P. Morgan liked to be addressed as Pierpont, his mother's maiden name, which we will also do in this book.

When Pierpont was a young boy, his grandfather, Joseph Morgan, would take him to the Episcopal Church every Sunday. It was something Pierpont loved to do. While in church, his favorite activity was singing hymns along with the choir. He would sing loud and proud and feel elated at the end of every service.

At school, he had the natural characteristics of a leader and exhibited it among his fellow classmates. While he attended many schools and never stayed in one school for very long unlike most children, he learned how to acclimate quickly to each school. Whether he was in America or Europe, Pierpont was able to pick out his comrades and shun those who were of no use to him.

His father raised him with a very specific vision in mind. He wanted Pierpont to be a captain of commerce and industry.

Unfortunately, serious health problems impeded Pierpont's education and progress. As a child, he suffered from headaches and other illnesses that often confined him to his bed.

When he was forced to stay home and recover, he often played solitaire. It was against his grain to just sit around and do nothing. Even when he experienced a migraine, he would find it unacceptable to lie in bed and wait for it to pass. Solitaire became his ally against the pain and a companion during times of loneliness. In later years, it would also be a panacea for frayed nerves.

When Pierpont's health improved, he passed his time by attending exhibitions of art in some of the finest galleries in New York, London, and Paris.

Art touched his soul and chased the blues away. The prospect of attending a gallery or viewing art would instantly place him in better spirits only to be bested by the actual event. It could bring sunshine to Pierpont's internal demons, which would attack at a moment's notice.

His youthful exposure to art and artists made Pierpont an aficionado, which was further enhanced by his early foray into art collection.

By his death, his art collection was worth more than $45 million. That was in 1913. Not accounting for the appreciation in the intrinsic value of the art and just looking at the purchasing power of the currency today, this would now amount to $1.1 billion.

In 1848, when Pierpont was eleven years old, he entered the Hartford Public School and shortly afterward transferred to the Episcopal Academy in Cheshire, also in Connecticut. A few years later, in 1851, Pierpont entered the English

School of Boston. This school trained students for a life in the world of business.

Unfortunately for Pierpont's studies and his own future feelings, he was stricken with rheumatic fever in 1852. He was sent to the Azores to recover and returned to Boston to continue his work about a year later. This illness left him with one leg shorter than the other, causing him to limp for the rest of his life. This was the first source of insecurity that struck him, and he was only fifteen years old.

At this age, how a male interacts with those around him and sees himself in the mirror is critical for how he develops in his late teens. In Pierpont's case that was marred by his ailments and limp. It was compounded by his inability to play sports. In time, this lack of physical activity led to gaining weight and clumsy self-perception.

After Pierpont graduated from high school, his father sent him to a village in Switzerland, which was known as La Tour-de-Peilz in the canton of Vaud. He went there to attend the boarding school of Bellerive. He was a good student. By the time he left Bellerive, he could speak, read, and write French like a native Parisian, and he had exceptional math skills. He was so good in this subject that his professor was disappointed that Pierpont was not planning to pursue academia in math. His professor strongly believed that Pierpont would use his skills in math as a basis for a life of academia and research, but Pierpont and his father had other plans.

Pierpont then went to the German University of Göttingen. Junius wanted his son to see the world and learn from different academic settings rather than just grow limp from the boredom of a single source of knowledge.

After studying for six months at Göttingen, he could speak German very well and graduated with a degree in arts. He could converse in German about current affairs, finance, and art without the person he was speaking to ever realizing that he was not a native speaker, but he could speak even better in French. It may have been because Pierpont was a closet romantic, and the French language suited his poetic heart.

Being elected valedictorian of his class at Göttingen, he had prepared a speech that was designed to impress the faculty and his fellow students, but much to his chagrin, he made a linguistic faux pas in his speech. He mixed up his words, *and* instead of wishing his fellow classmates a long life, he wished them a life of misery.

His teenage life was not an accurate reflection of his childhood. As a child, he was bubbly, full of laughter, and infectious joy, but that changed when he became sick in his early teenage years. His sickness altered his physical appearance, which eroded his confidence, causing a negative effect on his social skills. All that compounded his propensity for seclusion.

While the sicknesses that plagued him relentlessly as a teenager led him to withdraw from an active social life, his mind wasn't affected. If anything, the lack of social exposure actually focused his mind.

That childish, happy disposition gave way to a serious demeanor and fiery animation just below the surface that was ready to surface at a moment's notice. The insecurity he endured fueled the embers, while his disappointment nursed his bitterness. In the tug of war between his insecurities, persistent limp, and frequent migraines, his self-confidence was marginal at best. His outward demeanor to those who were in his orbit seemed brusque on a good day and downright fiery on a bad.

Pierpont's father partnered with the infamous George Peabody and worked with him for his bank for thirteen years before Old Man Peabody retired and left the day-to-day business of the bank to Junius. Pierpont was seventeen at this point when Junius became a partner.

By 1857, Junius believed that it was time for Pierpont to begin his career. To start, Pierpont began his banking life in the London office of Peabody, Morgan, and Company. It was an entry-level job that was designed to familiarize him with the ropes and get his feet wet. Pierpont had just turned twenty.

With the introduction to the financial world behind him, Pierpont returned to New York in

1858, where he began working at the firm Duncan, Sherman and Company.

Duncan, Sherman, and Company was the U.S. representative of Peabody, Morgan, and Company. Pierpont was neither a partner nor a director of the company, but that didn't stop him from pulling off a rather ambitious transaction that no one expected or sanctioned.

A large shipment of Brazilian coffee beans had arrived in New Orleans without a buyer. Due to some transactional anomaly, the intended buyer had backed off the deal, and the cargo was stuck at port. Pierpont used funds from Duncan, Sherman, and Company to purchase the entire shipment at a deep discount without anyone's permission. He then sold the shipment to merchants and was able to make a substantial return on the quick investment. It was a high-risk move and could have resulted in a total loss if a buyer was not found in time.

The partners at the firm were not at all pleased by what Pierpont had done. Their displeasure at his unsanctioned actions came back to haunt him a few years later when he was up for promotion. They declined his promotion to partner.

With the coffee bean saga behind him, the surge of adrenalin, despite the reproach of his seniors at the bank, was an exhilarating feeling that propelled this young banker in search of the next deal. He had been bitten by the deal bug—a typical ailment of successful bankers.

Now feeling emboldened and confident by his success, Pierpont struck out on his own and opened his own bank, J.P. Morgan and Company. Not to be confused, this is not the bank that is now JPMorgan Chase. This was a small bank that soon fizzled into oblivion. One deal does not a banker make.

As he was exposed to more deals and more transactions, he saw a very different element of the world of finance. His math skills were a great strength in his aptitude for banking. His ability to put the numbers together in his head made him a legend in his field. As he learned the ropes, the Morgan team of father and son found a new area of business that would eventually put them in the driver's seat in America's rise in the world.

The period between 1820 and the Civil War was one of significant consequence and opportunity for those who knew what to look for and what to go after. In the U.S., a new era of finance had developed. Gone were the days of basic banking where a dollar deposited in a bank was loaned out or invested by the banker. That was Banking 101.

Now things had to advance a little more, and other sources of funds needed to be found. Peabody had started that trend by bringing in money for sovereign bonds. Now the Morgans needed to do more. Junius was up to it but had his limits. Pierpont, on the other hand, was a little more brash and a lot more headstrong. He wanted to forge ahead with ideas that were yet to be tried and methods that were not yet tested. This worried Junius, who was a lot more conservative a banker than his son.

This difference of opinion caused constant rifts between the two, with the frustration coming to a boil in the younger Morgan, while the older Morgan was not as feisty.

Pierpont and his father worked to funnel British capital into the United States. In the 1830s and the 1840s, investors in Europe and Britain were wary about investing money in ventures that were three thousand miles away. Thanks to what Pierpont and his father were doing, however, investors started to become more confident in sending their money across the Atlantic Ocean.

Pierpont knew without a doubt that industry could not be financed by just the seasonal cash flow of deposits that came into banks because farmers would deposit them at harvest. They needed a year-round source of funds and had to attract money from the old country, but the old country and old money were hesitant after the defaults of numerous states. They needed assurances of future creditworthiness. They found that assurance in the structures and promises that Morgan brought to the table.

By this time, Pierpont was a grown man with a mustache and a piercing stare. He spent long hours at work but found time to entertain himself and go to social gatherings. During this time, he began to mingle with the social elite, attending the parties of highly respected families. He was frequently a guest at several prominent New York families' homes.

At one party, Pierpont met Amelia Sturges, who would later become his wife. Pierpont was smitten at once and fell in love with her, or Mimi, as he called her. Amelia's mother was a talented pianist, and her father was a supporter of the Hudson River School of Artists.

The feeling between Mimi and Pierpont was mutual. She liked him, and he proceeded to sweep her off her feet. New York, the about-to-be financial capital of the world, had much to offer a young couple. They visited art galleries, took boat rides on the Hudson, and rode horses in the country.

Chapter 2 Early Life

Pierpont's affection and affability were abundant and obvious until he started to withdraw into himself, but the full extent to which he secluded himself and retired from social company was still some years away.

There was a bond between father and son. Junius adored Pierpont and cherished every success, every attempt at success, and the way Pierpont thought. As for the son, he looked to his father with great admiration and wrote to Junius at every opportunity when they were separated by the Atlantic. Much of the correspondence was work related, but they also shared many personal father/son letters.

Being a sentimental man, Junius saved every single letter and memo in a box in his cabinet. Upon his death in 1890, Pierpont had the solemn duty of clearing his father's office. He had no idea that Junius had saved his letters, but Pierpont was not like his father. He was not sentimental. When he found the letters, he burned almost all of them. Only a few remain today and are preserved in the archives of the Morgan Library and Museum in New York.

As aggressive as he was in investing his funds, he always did so prudently. The fact that he was never sentimental about things was a great source of strength and allowed him to transact in large numbers and with a clear-eyed view of the risks involved. One such instance occurred in 1861, when he financed what came to be known as the Hall Carbine Affair.

Five thousand outdated army rifles were in a government munitions depot. An arms dealer by the name of Arthur M. Eastman purchased the entire lot for $3.50 each, with the total price being $17,500. He then sold them to a Mr. Stevens who borrowed $20,000 from Pierpont and purchased all the rifles for $11 each. That came up $55,000. He had $30,000 of his own money to make the deal.

The rifles were then modified, improving their accuracy and range and shipped to Union Field General John C. Fremont, who was at the time leading troops in Missouri. He purchased the rifles for $22 each. The total price was $110,000. Pierpont walked away with $44,000 on an investment of $20,000—a profit of 110 percent.

At the time of the Civil War, Wall Street was filled with people wanting to make money from it. What Pierpont did regarding the Hall Carbine Affair was not illicit. He was the kind of person who saw the war as an opportunity to make money, but he did so without cheating or fleecing the government or anyone else. He did, however, seek to make a return on his investments, and there is nothing wrong with that.

A few years later after Gettysburg Pierpont was conscripted into the army, but he paid a substitute $300 to take his place. At the time, that was a common practice and perfectly legal to do. Pierpont would refer to his substitute as "the other Pierpont Morgan."

In 1861, Pierpont and Mimi were married.

By this point, they had known each other for three years, but the decision to wed was forced on them by fate. Mimi had been diagnosed with tuberculosis, which few people survived.

When Pierpont found out about her condition, he was greatly disturbed. He immediately proposed to her, and she hesitantly accepted. Pierpont wanted to do the right thing and marry the love of his life. He then set about to find a cure for Mimi.

Mimi was so weak that Pierpont had to carry her downstairs to where the ceremony was taking place and had to hold her up. After that, he carried her to a waiting carriage outside.

The couple spent their honeymoon in Algiers, Tunisia. Pierpont thought the warm, dry air of the North African desert would bring her back to health. He also hired the finest physicians to tend to her and bought birds to keep her company.

Mimi wrote to her mother about how dedicated Pierpont was, but despite his attempts to nurse her back to health, she passed away on February 17, 1862, approximately four months after their wedding.

Pierpont was devastated. Even though he knew she would die, he was extremely heartbroken when he returned to New York, where he continued his work.

Three years later Pierpont married Frances Louisa Tracy, daughter of Charles Tracy, who owned a law firm, on May 31, 1865. At first, Frances, Fanny as she was also called, was not very attracted to him, but after one year of pursuit, she married him.

Within their first year of marriage, the couple had their first child, Louisa Pierpont Morgan. Over the next couple of years, they had two daughters and a son, John Pierpont Morgan Jr., or Jack, as he was also called. Jack grew up to become the next head of the House of Morgan. His two daughters were Anne, who became a philanthropist, and Juliet

It was around this time that Pierpont purchased a Victorian mansion close to the Hudson River. By now, he was earning $75,000 a year, which would be equivalent to almost $1.2 million today. He owned two houses, had a family, and was just thirty-three years old.

It was at this time that Pierpont's health began to deteriorate. His migraines were getting worse, and he also had skin problems. When he eventually recovered, he was left with his trademark nose for the rest of his life.

The acne rosacea that he suffered from made his nose abnormally large. Furthermore, his nose was covered with dimples and bulges and was also purple in color.

All photographs taken of him that he posed for were touched up to make his nose look normal. A few photographs, however, show what his nose really looked like.

Pierpont hated being photographed so much that one picture shows him warding off a photographer with his cane, and he appears to be shouting.

In one photo taken of Pierpont in 1903, the photographer asked Pierpont to turn his head a little to the side. Being conscious of his abnormal nose, however, he did not want to turn his head and simply stared straight into the camera.

It was at this time that he actually thought of retiring, but his father was not going to let that happen and made him work at the New York banking house of the Drexels. He became a partner of the bank in 1871, and the name was rechristened Drexel, Morgan, and Company. Junius also asked the owner of the bank, Anthony J. Drexel, to be a guide and mentor to Pierpont.

Although he was now at Drexel's firm, Pierpont was still a partner at Dabney, Morgan, and Company, where he had begun working in 1864. The owner of the bank, Charles Dabney, tutored Pierpont, and he was able to understand the way the chaotic banking system worked.

Pierpont actually continued at the firm of Dabney, Morgan, and Company until 1872, the year after he joined Drexel's firm.

As time went by, the relationship between Pierpont and Fanny began to sour. They were very different people, each of them liking different things. Pierpont loved luxurious furniture and clothes, while she just liked normal things. When Pierpont wanted to renovate their home, she told a friend that she hoped he wouldn't make their home too flamboyant.

For Fanny, she just liked pictures on the wall, thinking that it wouldn't be so attractive to thieves.

Pierpont would often go off with friends and would not return for months. He had several extramarital affairs, but only two were important.

Pierpont's son, Jack, would be the one who really spent time with Fanny. The two would bond over their depression, and when Fanny became somewhat deaf, he was there for her.

Jack was the exact opposite of Pierpont. When Pierpont was young and even when he grew old, he was always very ambitious, fearless, and aggressive. In contrast, Jack was a timid, reserved young boy with little self-confidence.

Pierpont was fond of Jack, but because he was not as active and enthusiastic as Pierpont was, Pierpont excluded him from business deals and for the better part of their time together kept him in the dark on transactions. When Pierpont formed United States Steel Corporation, Jack had to read about it in the newspapers. Because Pierpont excluded his son from the business, Jack felt even more insecure, which just dug the hole deeper.

Pierpont had a minor quirk concerning extramarital affairs. He always kept them private but rebuked those who were not discreet. He once called a young partner into his office and censured him for having had an affair. The young man replied, "But sir, you and the other partners do the same thing yourselves behind closed doors." Pierpont stared at him for a moment and then said, "Young man, that is what doors are for."

Despite his affairs, Pierpont always showed a great deal of respect to Fanny. He kept his affairs very quiet but took his mistresses out with him. He surrounded himself with people whom he trusted not to speak about the matter. When biographer Jean Strouse was researching his life, she talked to the children of the people who had kept Pierpont's affairs secret, and they, too, remained silent, as their parents who were friends with Pierpont did.

Pierpont's friends kept his affairs secret, but other associates were not completely secretive. They wrote down things, and some even spoke about the matter. Later in life, Pierpont himself did not completely cover up his affairs out of complacency and thinking they would not be found out. It was not possible, however, to keep them a complete secret forever. The press and the public were constantly hammering Pierpont, and it was impossible for them not to see some of the skeletons in his not completely closed closet.

There was a lot for Morgan to be angry about. His affairs were indicative of that. In fact, although he was affectionate toward Fanny, the true love of his life was Mimi. He had no intention of marrying after her death, but Junius had insisted that he get over her.

In fact, it was Junius who arranged for and cajoled Pierpont into the meeting with Fanny and the subsequent courtship. Neither Pierpont nor Fanny was interested in the idea.

Pierpont's heart was broken when Mimi died. Many people said that her death haunted him to his final days.

What complicated everything was that the son he loved was the product of a union that didn't matter to him. He treated Fanny with the utmost respect and kept his affairs away from her as a sign of that respect. Once she retreated to her room upstairs and led a silent life, he knew there was not much he could do to win her back, so the need to be discreet was no longer as great as it had been. Even in his indiscretions, though, he was still a gentleman.

Chapter 3 Shortcomings

Pierpont's son-in-law, the husband of Louisa Pierpont Morgan, Herbert L. Satterlee, said that perhaps Pierpont did not fix his nose because he did not want the seizures he used to suffer from when he was young to return. Doctors could actually have shaved away the cauliflower-like part of his nose so that it would be normal, but that didn't happen.

The condition of his nose contributed to his hostile personality, which resulted from deep-seated insecurity. Pierpont had two issues that to him were at odds with each other. His life started out with intense seizures. These were debilitating and scary for him when he was young. It shook him to his core. The seizures became increasingly violent and would last longer as he grew older.

At about the same time the seizures stopped, the rosacea erupted on his face and centered on his nose. Rosacea is an inflammatory condition that typically affects the face but can spread to the upper torso as well. It alters the tint of the skin just as a serious case of acne would. In Pierpont's case, the buildup of fluid and white cells in his nose altered its shape and deformed its appearance. The more enraged Pierpont became, the brighter his nose would glow.

Because the Rosacea developed about the same time his seizures stopped, Pierpont associated one with the other. In his mind, fixing his nose, which the doctors assured him could be done, would cause the seizures to resurface. There was no medical evidence of that, but he believed it.

The more his nose grew, the more it preoccupied him until he hardly looked at the mirror except to groom himself. Just as how one can affirm the strength of their psyche by looking at themselves in the mirror, Pierpont had the opposite effect. Each visit to the mirror in the morning was a painful reminder of what greeted the rest of the world. He wanted no record of it, and he didn't like it when people stared at it. Everyone in his office knew better than to look at his nose.

Pierpont was aggressive in his temperament when he didn't want to be photographed. He didn't just stop at that though. If someone said something about his nose, he would do something to get back at them. He never let it go.

When someone once nicknamed him "Livernose," Pierpont banned that person from joining the New York Yacht Club, a club in which he was a member. When Pierpont was once visiting the family of an associate, the man's wife told her children not to say anything about his nose. She had warned them since she knew they had never met Pierpont and would be distracted by his nose. Little did she realize that she herself was so preoccupied with it that it caused an inadvertent slip of the tongue. Once Pierpont arrived and she was serving tea, she blurted out, "Do you like a nose in your tea, Mr. Morgan?"

Despite his state of mind about his nose, he held his composure and dignity when meeting people. He was no doubt fully aware that they were staring at his nose, and he didn't like it one bit, but his propensity to do the deal outweighed his discomfort. Some close to him believe that his shroud of cigar smoke was a means to obscure the sight of his bulbous nose. This shroud or aromatic cloud that hovered around him perpetually was a trait that became synonymous with Pierpont's personal brand. He used to smoke almost twenty full-sized cigars a day, with Cubans being his favorite, especially the eight-inch Maduro Meridiana Kohinoor cigars also known as "Hercules' Clubs." He smoked so much that you could sniff him coming around the corner, and his presence was unmistakable once he was gone.

In his private life, Pierpont was a deeply devout Christian, who was loyal to the Episcopal Church. It had been that way since he was a child and shepherded to Episcopal services by his grandfather.

As he matured, the foundation of the church and the teachings of the Bible had a significant bearing on his mind and beliefs. He believed every single thing in the Bible and said he believed the story of Jonah and the whale. Most of us understand that the parables in the Bible are instructional. They have their value and are powerful in their representation, but not many believe the parables to be literal and historically accurate. As intelligent and sharp as Pierpont was, he saw the church as more than what most people view it to be.

He was such a devout Christian that he would frequently go for walks and end up at a church. It would be empty, and he would just stand there and commune with God. He would stand there in obvious prayer and then burst into song, singing his medley of favorite hymns. Pierpont would be absolutely mesmerized by the church, both its edifice and its teachings. He was a very pious man in mind, spirit, and action. He made numerous contributions to the church.

Aside from simply being a pious Christian, Pierpont was also involved in the church. He had been both a member of the Episcopal Church and was one time an important leader of the church. Pierpont was also one of the founders of the Church Club of New York, which was an Episcopal club. He also donated $100,000 to help Bishop Charles Brent's idea to come true.

Bishop Brent wanted churches from all over the world to meet and discuss their differences regarding "faith and order." He wanted a

General Convention of the Episcopal Church. Pierpont loved the idea very much, which is why he provided financial support.

Chapter 4 Early Deals

In 1879, Pierpont was approached by William Vanderbilt, the son of Cornelius Vanderbilt, who wanted to sell 250,000 shares of the New York Central Railroad.

Vanderbilt could have gone to any competent broker to find the best price and a buyer in a short amount of time, but he had larger concerns. Vanderbilt wanted to make sure that two things were adhered to: (1) that the sale was done discreetly. It had to be done in such a way that the Vanderbilt name did not enter the papers for selling some of their shares, and (2) the sale had to be done in a way that did not affect the price of the shares and the market in general.

It was a large transaction, yet Pierpont was able to pull it off without causing the stock price to fall or the information to become public The maneuver took skill and facility with the ways of the stock market—both of which Pierpont was very skilled at doing. The consideration for this transaction did not stop at fees as with an ordinary transaction. This was extraordinary in nature and deserved extraordinary compensation. In the world of corporate finance and trading, mobilizing large amounts of cash for the purchase of a single stock was not easy, and doing it without shaking the stock price required seismic force and a general touch, which only Pierpont could do at the time.

In return for his service, Pierpont boldly requested and received a directorship position on the board of the New York Central Railway.

Fortune had smiled on Pierpont, and he had taken full advantage of it. He now had jammed his foot in the door of the railroad industry.

Without wasting any time, Pierpont set off another project, which involved raising $40 million through a bond issuance for the construction of the Northern Pacific Railroad from Minnesota to Oregon. To put that in context, $40 million then is equivalent to $1.2 billion today. At the time, it was the largest bond issuance and placement in the history of the United States. Pierpont was not in it to play small. He was geared to play with big dollar amounts, which showed his prowess, intelligence, and ability.

Pierpont was also involved in other major projects. We all turn on the lights in our houses and never for a moment think what it was like before Edison invented the light bulb. It was not very bright then and had a foul stench. The burning of whale blubber or poorly refined kerosene imparted an odious tinge on everything, from one's clothes to one's furniture. It wasn't until the arrival of the light bulb and wired-in electricity that the flip of a switch illuminated the room. It wasn't just Edison who was behind that. Edison certainly improved the design of the bulb, made it work, and then developed the switches, fuse, wires, and cables as well as the power generation stations behind the whole affair of light at the flick of a switch, but behind Edison stood J.P. Morgan, the man who had financed it. Pierpont was the man behind electricity generation and the bulb becoming widely used across the United States.

After Edison perfected the light bulb and the infrastructure behind it, Pierpont had him install electricity in his home at 219 Madison Avenue. A small generator was installed to supply power to the four hundred light bulbs in the house. This same home became a place where Edison conducted his experiments.

Pierpont's father thought it was a waste of time, but electricity soon became a necessity in the homes of well-to-do people.

Pierpont invested a great deal of money in Edison and financed the forming of the Edison Electricity Company. The first power station ever to exist was then created, and half of Manhattan Island had access to electricity. Although this was a splendid success for Pierpont and Edison, it was a great loss for John D. Rockefeller.

Before the rise of electricity, Rockefeller supplied oil to people who had lamps that used oil for power. With his market for oil now reduced, he resorted to fabricating dangers about electricity. He gave these false stories to the newspapers, letting this information spread among the public.

In 1889, the firm of Drexel, Morgan, and Company bankrolled Edison and helped Edison's companies to merge, forming the Edison General Electric Company on April 24, 1889. The companies included in the merger were the Edison Machine Works, the Edison Lamp Company, and the Edison Electric Light Company. In the same year, the Sprague Electric Railway and Motor Company were brought into the company.

Eleven years after Pierpont dealt with William Vanderbilt, Junius Morgan passed away in Monte Carlo. Pierpont and his family had visited him the year before and spent their last summer with the patriarch of the Morgan clan. At that point, Junius had aged, and not much of his spark as a lifelong banker remained. He had become a grandfather excited to see his progeny. In April 1890, Junius went into a coma after an accident. The injuries from that accident precipitated and hastened his final days.

Three years later Anthony Joseph Drexel, founder of Drexel, Morgan, and Company, passed away, leaving the company to Pierpont, who unceremoniously renamed the firm two years later to J.P. Morgan and Company. This firm would become one of the largest banks in the world as well as what is today known as JPMorgan Chase and Company.

Following this rechristening, Pierpont would keep his firm closely connected with the Drexel firm of Philadelphia and Paris. The Paris part of the firm was called Morgan, Harjes & Company, and the Philadelphia branch was called Drexel and Company. J.P. Morgan & Co. also stayed close to J.S. Morgan and Company, which would be renamed Morgan, Grenfell, and Company in 1910.

Chapter 5 The Peabody Effect

Morgan, Grenfell, and Company started as George Peabody and Company, founded by the banker scrooge and philanthropist George Peabody.

George Peabody was a patriotic American from the state of Massachusetts. He arrived in Britain in 1835 and shortly afterward opened his own merchant's dry goods store and furnished it with a safe and some tables. He formed a merchant bank and named it George Peabody and Company. This little merchant bank functioned as a firm that dealt only with rich people, large companies, and governments. He was very proud of his country, and rather than just going about his business and being part of British society, he stood out as an American, spreading the popularity of American goods and showing how good they were.

His claim to fame and success came about in the wake of one of America's shameful moments. After the issuance of numerous bonds for development and floating those bonds to Europe, a number of states that floated bonds, including Indiana, Michigan, Pennsylvania, Arkansas, and the territory of Florida, defaulted on their interest payments to the Bank of England and other private banking houses in 1841 and 1842. This deepened the recession that had been sparked by other factors and prolonged by the famine that hit Ireland and Scotland.

Several American state governors came together and tried to repudiate the remaining debt, but it did not work. Even today the state of Mississippi is still in debt from the 1840s.

British investors were extremely disgusted by what had happened and considered the United States to be an untrustworthy country, filled with people who did not fulfill their end of a bargain.

Since states were defaulting on their debt, the federal credit rating fell. Thus, in 1842 when President John Tyler sent Treasury representatives to Europe, French banker James Mayer de Rothschild said, "Tell them you have seen the man who is at the head of the finances of Europe, and that he has told you that they cannot borrow a dollar. Not a dollar."

Several other people also looked on with disdain with what had happened in the States. One such person was Sydney Smith, a clergyman. He said he felt an urge to "seize and divide him" when he saw a man of Pennsylvania sitting down at a dinner in London. He went on to say, "How such a man can set himself down at an English table without feeling that he owes two or three pounds to every man in the company, I am at a loss to conceive; he has no more right to eat with honest men than a leper has to eat with clean men."

Author Charles Dickens was also disgusted with the Americans. In one of his stories, one of his characters has British assets that are turned into as he puts it, "a mere United States' security."

Needless to say, the entire affair was a dark stain on Americans and this country. The state of Maryland would later join the long list of defaulters as well. Peabody felt very passionate about this particular issue and said that whenever he met a British investor he would be embarrassed.

The defaulting of Pennsylvania and Maryland was the most upsetting for the British because these states were tied to Anglo-Saxon stock.

The person behind much of the sale of bonds to the European banking houses and investors was none other than George Peabody, Junius Morgan's banking partner.

Peabody had sold approximately half of Maryland's shares to European investors, which caused some trouble for him when they eventually defaulted. He became the face of the defaulters since he was personally in London.

Although the *London Times* described Peabody as an "American gentleman of the most unblemished character," he was rejected by the Reform Club because he was from the United States, which defaulted on its debts. It was a hard time for Peabody because he was proud of his American heritage. When the defaults started and then deepened, he was still in London and was called upon to explain what had happened.

Peabody later wrote to a friend, saying, "You and I will, I trust, see that happy day, when as formerly, we can own ourselves Americans in Europe, without a blush for the character of our Country."

This showed how Peabody had been affected. He was evidently very proud of the United States, and this shameful episode was almost unbearable.

He finally had to take matters into his own hands to get some of the states to pay their dues. He had a novel idea that was similar to public relations. Peabody paid reporters to write favorable stories about Maryland. In 1845, Peabody teamed up with Barings to get Maryland to continue paying its debt. The two of them organized a slush fund that was to be used to promote the idea of continuing to pay its debts.

Peabody even peruaded clergymen to deliver speeches talking about the "holiness" of contracts.

From a secret account that Peabody and Barings maintained, they gave one thousand pounds to Baltimore, nine hundred of which came from Barings, while the remaining one hundred came from Peabody. Barings would later enact this scheme for Pennsylvania. Peabody wasn't the only one paying people to promote creditworthiness. Barings paid a speaker as well as the prominent political figure Daniel Webster to promote the idea of paying debts in his talks.

Just because Peabody and Barings were operating in a questionable way by paying people to promote things in the background did not mean they were all right with it. In fact, they did not like what they were doing even if it was not illegal but did feel a little underhanded.

Joshua Bates, a senior partner of the Barings, said to the American Thomas Ward, "Your payment to Mr. Webster would not appear very well if it should get out." Thomas Ward was the man who collected the money for Peabody and

Barings' operation. Bates acted very by the book and was a clean "recorded" man who did not look favorably upon Peabody's exploits. He said, "I have a sort of instinctive horror of doing one thing to affect another, or using any sort of subterfuge or reserve."

Despite the questionability of the operation, it was successful. Whigs who favored states to repay their debts were elected in both Pennsylvania and Maryland. The English bankers in London once again received their regular payments from those two states. The states of Mississippi and Florida, however, did not repay their debts.

To go on, just know that Peabody was the kind of person that if you stung him he would sting you back. Now, Mississippi and Florida obviously did not do anything to hurt Peabody except that they hurt his pride for his country by not paying their debts and causing the Victorian bankers of Britain to look at Americans with contempt and disdain. In his later years when Peabody donated to charity and presented gifts to the country, he refrained from giving anything to

Mississippi and Florida because they had brought him such shame.

This was not entirely an altruistic move hoping to raise his country's worth in the eyes of Europeans. He had made heavy bets by buying up the junk bonds that ewe in the market for pennies on the dollar.

Junk bonds are bonds rated below investment grade. It means they have defaulted on one or more of their payments and have been downgraded by a rating agency. In the case of the state bonds, there were no rating agencies at the time, but they did indeed default, and as such those who were holding the bonds needed to sell as many as they could to recover as much capital as they could. Peabody was one of few who bought up those bonds at a deeply discounted price.

Once he had succeeded in getting a number of states to pay and the bonds rose in value, he made a fortune.

In time, thanks to his efforts, American bonds soon became much more secure than those of

Europe because of the many revolutions that took place in Europe in 1848 and that America was developing and advancing at a pace that was significantly greater than all of the Old World combined.

As the 1840s drew to a close, the Mexican War and the California Gold Rush brought an end to the tumultuous '40s, and Peabody was once again able to hold his head high as he walked the streets of London. He considered himself to be the bridge that brought American culture to Victorian Britain. He presented the English nation with apples of his country, hominy grit, and crackers of Boston.

Peabody's first Independence Day dinner took place on July 4, 1851. At the celebration, the most important guest was Arthur Wellesley, the Duke of Wellington.

Through his actions, Peabody was trying to stitch together friendship between the British and the Americans, but it didn't all go as well as he had hoped. In 1854, Peabody did something that was considered heretical. In this case, however, it was not heretical for the church but for the American government. Peabody had toasted to Queen Victoria before he did for Franklin Pierce, president of the United States at the time. James Buchanan, who was the American ambassador to London and would be the next U.S. president, was upset and immediately left the room. It was a small matter, and Buchanan was indeed acting impetuously.

Peabody also took up the role of showing Americans around London. He took some eighty Americans to dinner and thirty-five to the opera.

When Cornelius Vanderbilt came to London with his wife and all twelve children in tow in 1853, Peabody showed him around.

Commodore Vanderbilt came to Britain to show how great America was since a poor boy could now be richer than the queen. He arrived in his yacht, the *North Star*, a ship that weighed two thousand tons. On board besides himself and his family were a doctor, a caterer, and a chaplain.

In the 1850s, Peabody earned quite a bit of money supplying the United States with railroad rails and financing the silk trade that was taking place with China. Peabody did help some charities, but mostly he accumulated money to have a reserve if a financial crisis occurred.

The small acts of charity included building a library for a secondary education school.

As Peabody made more money, he became more obsessed that he might lose it. He once told an associate that he had a great deal of money and had seen large sums of money lost in financial panics. He went on to say that he had to be careful with his fortune.

Thomas Perman, Peabody's assistant, really seemed to dislike him and gave an account of his "dark" side. He recounted a story about how Peabody used to eat his lunch at his desk every day. He went on to say how he would send a clerk to buy an apple for him, which cost one and a halfpenny. Peabody would give the young man two pence. The clerk wished to be able to keep the halfpenny as a little bonus for himself, but Peabody would not hear of it. He always wanted his change back.

At the beginning of the 1850s, Peabody's health was not too good. He would soon wish to commit himself to charity, but another problem would delay his plans.

By this time, Peabody earned $300,000 a year but only spent $3,000 of it. He was very rich but spent very little. Peabody never married, but he did have an illegitimate daughter, whose mother would frequently receive two thousand pounds from him.

When the daughter grew up, she would constantly pester the Morgan family for money, for Peabody had left nothing for either her or her mother in his will. No one knows why Peabody was so out of touch regarding family matters, but he had "telescopic philanthropy," a term created by Charles Dickens. Telescopic philanthropy simply means that one is kind and loves humanity as a whole but is very unkind and hurtful to individuals he knows.

The world, or more specifically the English would, considered him a benevolent man, but his employees and illegitimate family felt otherwise.

Problems arose when the time came for Peabody to leave the banking business and shift his focus to philanthropy. Although he was master of his own bank, no one else knew enough of the bank's operations to be able to continue in his absence.

Because he had no other choice, Peabody appointed Charles C. Gooch to be a junior partner, hoping that Gooch would then ascend to a position of control. Before holding this position, Gooch was Peabody's office manager. So the fit was just not there to transition from an inward role to one that oversaw everything.

It was never the practice in nineteenth century banking houses for strangers to take over after the incumbent head passed away or retired. They typically passed to an heir. This time, however, Peabody was in the position of having no son to pass on his business. Thus, he had to fish for someone to take over.

Peabody had certain conditions for the man who would take over George Peabody and Company: be an American with a family and have experience in international trade. Furthermore, that American must be a man that could *talk—be a master communicator*—and mingle with other people.

Peabody knew a James Beebe who owned the firm J.M. Beebe and Morgan. He told Peabody about Junius Spencer Morgan, his junior partner. Junius had been with J.M. Beebe for three years. Beebe praised Junius, who was indeed an astute and intelligent individual. He was a true blue-blooded American.

Peabody wanted to see him, so Junius took his family with him to London to meet Peabody in May 1853. Junius brought along his son, John Pierpont Morgan Sr., who was very excited about his first time in Britain. While his father met with Peabody, Pierpont visited Westminster Abbey and the queen's residence, Buckingham Palace. Pierpont also attended a Sunday morning session at the church of St. Paul's.

Junius Spencer Morgan was a very clean, neat, and by-the-book banker. He gave Pierpont a lot of advice and always stood there telling him what to do and what not to do. In Junius' eyes, Pierpont was rash and undisciplined, which worried him. An example of what his father foresaw includes how Pierpont bought an entire shipment of Brazilian coffee with the money of the firm he was working in, which bothered all the senior bankers at the time.

After talking for a few days and assessing this young banker, Peabody asked him to become his partner. They were two very different men. One was an American but had lived his entire life in the Old World, while the other was a dyed-in-the-wool American, who had spent most of his life in the New World. One was a seasoned banker; the other was a novice. One had no family, and the other was a family man by nature. And, since opposites attract, there was a bond that formed between them across the generational divide. The conversation that ensued was kept alive by the generations of Morgans that recounted the event to their children.

Peabody began, "You know, I shall not want to go on much longer, but if you will come as a partner for ten years, I shall retire at the end of them, and at that time shall be willing to leave my name, and, if you have not accumulated a reasonable amount of capital in the concern, some of my money also, and you can go ahead as the head of it."

Junius replied by saying, "Well, Mr. Peabody, that sounds like a very good offer, but there are many things to be considered, and I could not think of giving an answer until I have looked over the books of the firm and have some idea of the business and of the methods by which it is done."

This was evidence that Junius wasn't overexcited at the prospect of becoming a partner of George Peabody and Company—not that he wasn't interested, but that he wasn't the kind of person to immediately jump into something. Junius first wanted to see how well the firm did before he made up his mind.

When Junius saw that the firm of George Peabody and Company had 450,000 pounds, he was deeply impressed. This placed Peabody's firm just behind the Rothschild and Baring houses.

In October 1854, Junius Spencer Morgan agreed to become the partner of George Peabody and Company and took up his office at 22 Old Broad Street.

When Junius moved in, he didn't make any renovations because it wasn't necessary. It was good as it was, and it made no sense to spend hard-earned money on mere renovations. True bankers are traditionally a miserly lot.

When Junius Spencer Morgan became Peabody's partner and moved to London, it was a bit of a nicer time for a banker from the United States in London than when Peabody started there. The Crimean War was going on at the time, and the price of American grain had risen. Railroad companies with lines in the western part of the country were transporting supplies and making money from there, causing many people to want to own shares of these railroads.

A contract between Peabody and his newly minted partner specified what Peabody's firm would do, which included international trade, purchasing and selling stocks, and buying railroad building materials as well as other items on behalf of others. Peabody also gave Junius a budget of 2,500 pounds to amuse visiting Americans.

Ten years after the two men became partners, Junius confronted him about what he had promised when they became partners. Junius would then be in the same group of people that had been pushed aside in an unfair and contemptuous manner.

During their partnership, Junius once found his partner sitting in a countinghouse looking most sickly. He advised Peabody that he should go home, and Peabody agreed. Later, Junius saw his partner standing in the rain and asked him why he did not go home. Peabody replied by saying that a bus had come, but that it was a two-pence bus, and he was waiting for one that cost one pence.

Although he owned a company with 450,000 pounds as capital and earned 300,000 a year with a total wealth of approximately a million pounds, George Peabody was very stingy with his spending. He once marched a cab driver down to the police station for overcharging him.

Most bankers have the same psychology: make lots, spend little.

Peabody's firm was one of the most prominent railroad share dealers in London and thus able to benefit nicely from the frenzy of railroad activity in the United States. Railroad companies in the U.S., while starting off slowly, were now earning so much money that they had gained the interest of many investors. During the Civil War, many investors invested a total of $1 billion in railroads, and Junius was the face of that activity in London.

Between 1854 and 1864, Junius wondered whether or not it was the right decision to move to London and become Peabody's partner. Peabody was not easy to deal with, and their relationship had turned rather cold. Whenever Junius wrote to Peabody, he would begin with "Dear Sir" and end the letter "J.S. Morgan."

Junius' opinion of Peabody was that he was spiteful and revengeful. The two were not really very friendly in later years and only showed each other their due respect and courtesy.

Three years after Junius and Peabody became partners, wheat prices fell when the Crimean War ended. This was a serious problem for both American banking houses as well as the railroad companies, which no longer had such a large customer demanding shipments of grain.

In October 1857, American banks in New York ceased paying in gold, which stopped Peabody from receiving funds in London, and he could not pay his obligations. It was soon suspected that Peabody's firm would collapse much to his competitors' delight. Like Junius, many people did not like old man Peabody.

Some of the larger London banking houses approached Junius and told him that they would help the firm of Peabody, Morgan, and Company pay off its debts under the condition that Peabody closed the bank within a year.

Junius relayed the message to Peabody who strenuously refused. He was adamant in his resolve to not shutter his bank.

In an unexpected turn of events, the firm received an offer of a loan from the Bank of

England for 800,000 pounds. The loan was guaranteed by the House of Baring.

Peabody felt entrapped and directed his frustrations toward Baring. The entire issue of the financial crisis was very painful for him.

When Pierpont learned that the bank his father was a partner in was going to renege on its loans, he was quite upset.

This financial juggernaut greatly affected Junius and altered his methods of banking. He became significantly more cautious.

He also started to lecture his son to walk safely in the line of business his son was working in, as he was also starting his banking career.

He once wrote Pierpont, "You are commencing upon your business career at an eventful time. Let what you now witness make an impression not to be eradicated . . . *slow and sure* should be the motto of every young man."

Since 1832 when President Andrew Jackson dissolved the Bank of the United States, the nation had no standard way of banking. Furthermore, there were quite a number of places in which people did not have to pay their debts with the dollar but could use the currencies of other countries.

Soon, another financial issue was brewing. The merchant banks in London began to take equity stakes, one example being when Peabody's firm invested 100,000 pounds in the creation of Cyrus Field's transatlantic communication cable from London to New York. It was proved a success on August 15, 1858, when Queen Victoria sent a telegram to President James Buchanan by the transatlantic cable.

For the next two weeks, everyone in New York was celebrating, and the skies were filled with fireworks.

Peabody then wrote to Field, saying, "Your reflections must be like those of Columbus after the discovery of America." Peabody was evidently happy about this new transatlantic cable. Unfortunately, however, the cable broke, and the company's share prices dropped dramatically. The firm of George Peabody and Company as well as Junius and Peabody themselves lost a lot of money. The cable would only be restored eight years later.

Peabody may have remained at the bank until 1864, but from 1859 until then, he was only a figurehead. Junius had already taken control of the bank in 1859.

During the Civil War, Junius traded Union bonds, the value of which changed whenever Union troops either lost or won a battle.

When the Confederates defeated the Union troops at the Battle of Bull Run, Union bonds reduced dramatically but increased dramatically when the Confederates were brought to a halt at Antietam Creek. Vicksburg, Confederate territory, was taken by the Union in July 1863, and Junius' son, Pierpont, wrote to his father through the telegram cable the Nova Scotia and told him about the Union victory. Junius was informed early enough to make a nice profit from American bonds.

This sort of banking was, as historian Ron Chernow put it, "calamity banking," and in the realm of merchant banks, it was quite prevalent.

One of the Rothschild bankers said, "When the streets of Paris are running with blood, I buy." This basically meant that they, too, participated in "calamity banking."

At one point in the Civil War, President Abraham Lincoln needed money to pay for the war debt and approached Jay Cooke, a Philadelphia banker. Cooke sent his people to sell war bonds, and the Jewish bankers of German nationality operating from Wall Street were thrown into a frenzy. Among the London buyers was Peabody's firm.

George Peabody went through a change during the Civil War. Before the war, he was a stingy, unlikeable banker whose only focus was making and hoarding money. After the Civil War, however, he became very generous, although he could not fully wrest himself of the habits he had when he used to hoard his money. He said, "It is not easy to part with the wealth we have accumulated after years of hard work and difficulty."

One distinct difference between Peabody and the Morgans and more specifically Pierpont was that

Peabody came from nothing. He had no inherited wealth or family that was wealthy. He started off with nothing and worked his way up to become extremely rich and the father of modern philanthropy. The quality of saving in a person comes from when that person starts off with nothing and goes on to become rich from his or her own hard work.

Pierpont's family was already rich. He grew up surrounded by luxury and had the gift to do anything he wanted right then and there. This rich background did not instill in him the necessity to save, and when Pierpont grew up and amassed his own wealth, he was not miserly or frugal with it one bit. He spent lavishly on cigars, yachts, parties, and his art and gem collections. Pierpont died a fairly wealthy man, but John D. Rockefeller allegedly remarked, "And to think, he wasn't even a rich man." His wealth in today's world is a lot of money, but compared with Rockefeller's $300 billion and Andrew Carnegie's wealth, Pierpont's forty-one is actually very little. That did not matter, though, for his success was still paramount—

more than his wealth. His success was also more important than the amount of money he had. It was also said that his power was not based on the millions he had, but with the billions he dealt with.

Coming from a rich background is beneficial. It allows you to have all the resources you need and be able to achieve your success in comfort and not have to worry about monetary issues. For Peabody, he had to struggle just to sustain himself and had to work hard to amass his wealth.

He had been saving his money his entire life, and now he was going to spend lavishly through his philanthropy. In 1857, Peabody funded the Peabody Institute in Baltimore. When Pierpont or the Morgan family later did their philanthropy, they did it for the purpose of giving to charity and doing good for the people. They did their charity work anonymously and very calmly. Peabody, however, wanted to be known for his philanthropy. He wanted his name attached to every single thing he funded or endowed. In 1862, Peabody deposited 150,000 pounds into a trust fund, the purpose of which was to build homes for London's poor. These houses, known as Peabody Estates, were nicely furnished with a water supply and gas lamps. They are still standing today.

As a reward for his outstanding benevolence, he was awarded the Freedom of the City of London, the first American as well as the first person who was not British to ever be given that award. When Peabody was having dinner at a mansion, he said, "From a full and grateful heart, I say that this day has repaid me for the care and anxiety of fifty years of commercial life."

Peabody's philanthropy was very impressive during his final years. He funded Yale University's natural history museum and Harvard University's ethnology museum. He also contributed to an educational fund dedicated to former slaves.

Requests for more homes amounted to a total cost of 500,000 pounds. As he was so generous, people started to take a more godly view of him. Victor Hugo, author of *Lès Miserables,* said, "On this earth, there are men of hate and men of love. Peabody was one of the latter. It is on the face of these men that we see the smile of God."

William E. Gladstone remarked that Peabody was able to impress upon people how to use money, not be controlled by it.

Queen Victoria offered Peabody a noble title. He could choose to become either a knighthood or a baron, but Peabody refused. Seeing that he would not accept either position, she simply wrote a letter to the poor of London, writing "princely munificence" in regards to Peabody. Although Peabody was busy providing for the people, he never did anything for his partner and heir, Junius Spencer Morgan. Perhaps this is a case where telescopic philanthropy applies.

In 1864, the time came for Peabody to retire and for Junius to become head of the bank. He had actually already been its head but would now also become known as its leader. Peabody had promised ten years earlier to leave his name with the bank, and if Junius had not accumulated enough money to run the firm, to leave some of his own. Peabody did neither of those things. Junius was deeply disappointed by Peabody's decision. It was then that the firm of George Peabody and Company was named J.S. Morgan and Company. Junius, however, was not very happy. In 1910, it would be renamed once more and be called Morgan, Grenfell, and Company.

Junius was left as the owner and head of the bank.

He was forced by Peabody to buy the office he had worked in that was on 22 Old Broad Street at the end of the ten-year partnership. Peabody demanded that he buy it and gave him very difficult terms and conditions. The grandson of Junius Morgan, Jack, wrote that Junius said that Peabody used to be difficult regarding the price of the office. Junius had been very angry with Peabody but had calmed down because while he was at George Peabody and Co. the firm had earned 444,000 pounds, which had been divided between him and Peabody. Junius was also happy to have taken ownership of the most prominent American banking firm in London, home of British banking firms.

Peabody passed away five years after he retired from George Peabody and Company. He was seventy-four years old. A temporary grave at Westminster Abbey was dug by the British government.

A statue of George Peabody was unveiled behind the Royal Exchange by Edward VII, then Prince of Wales. This was a rare gesture considering the cramped space of the city. When Peabody was alive, he had worked to establish peace and friendship between the United States and Britain. At the time of his death, the British completed construction of a new warship, an extremely powerful vessel that stirred anxiety in the United States. In the end, however, the ship would be used for peace. Steel tycoon Andrew Carnegie sent a telegram to John Bright, who was then part of the British Cabinet. He wrote, "First and best service possible for *Monarch*, bringing home body Peabody." Andrew Carnegie wrote the message anonymously. Soon afterward, Queen Victoria called for the *HMS Monarch* to be used as the transport vessel to take George Peabody's remains back to the United States. A makeshift funeral chapel was built on the ship. Peabody's coffin was covered with a black sheet, and candles burned in the room. U.S. Admiral Farragut and his men received the ship in the United States. Pierpont Morgan had been given the responsibility of handling the funeral, and he organized a little something for the old banker. He arranged for British and American soldiers to march behind the coffin.

His life even inspired Queen Victoria to pen a Royal letter for his service. It reads as follows:

"I have always understood that Mr. Peabody, though known as a great philanthropist, was one of the meanest men that ever walked. I do not know if you ever saw the statue of him sitting on a chair behind the Royal Exchange. Old Mr. Burns told me once that when subscriptions were invited in the City to erect a statue there was so little enthusiasm that there was not sufficient money to pay for the chair, and Mr. Peabody had to pay for it himself. When I first came here the head of our office was Mr. Perman, and I remember when he had been here sixty years Teddy [Grenfell] and I gave all the staff a dinner at the Saucy, and we took them to a Music hall afterward, and old Mr. Perman was at his desk at nine o'clock the next morning. He knew George Peabody's form well and used to tell Jack many stories . . . indicative of his meanness. I always understood that when he retired he announced he was leaving his money in the business—and at once proceeded to take it out. I believe he left several illegitimate children totally unprovided for."

This letter is quite strange for a letter meant to *thank* someone. It sounded more as if the queen were faulting or criticizing Peabody. It did, however, show that although Peabody was very generous in his philanthropy and a very successful man, he wasn't at all a nice person. But then again, not many nice people have succeeded in life.

If it hadn't been for Peabody, however, the fate of the Morgan household would be unknown at this point. It was Peabody who brought Junius in, and that allowed Pierpont to be exposed to some of the most interesting, historic, and pivotal events in the world of finance and the development of the United States. The life of

George Peabody is deeply entwined with that of the Morgans and by extension the House of Morgan that followed decades later.

Chapter 6 Jack Morgan

In 1898, when Jack Morgan was already thirty-one years old, he was working at J.S. Morgan and Company. He, too, had a big nose, but it was nowhere near the size of his father's. Jack learned about what had happened in New York and wanted a piece of the action. He once said to his mother, ". . . when I think of home the time does seem a bit long," indicating that he missed New York, the hub of chaos and American banking.

Jack wasn't comfortable with sitting in a very calm place watching the fun happen three thousand miles away on the other side of the Atlantic Ocean. What he felt more upset about was that Robert Bacon was being favored by his father over him. Robert Bacon was, for a short period of time, the Secretary of State under Theodore Roosevelt. Bacon was also a prominent political person.

The plan was that Jack would be posted in London for a short time, but he would only return to the United States in 1905. In 1897, Mary Lyman Morgan's husband, Walter Hayes Burns of J.S. Morgan and Company, passed away. She was Pierpont's sister. He was replaced by Walter Spencer Morgan Burns, the son of Mary Lyman Morgan, Jack's cousin.

Following the passing of Walter Hayes Burns, more novices were in the firm of J.S. Morgan and Company than seasoned bankers.

Pierpont's niece, the daughter of Mary Lyman and Walter Hayes Burns and the sister of Walter Spencer Morgan Burns, married the first Viscount of Harcourt, Lewis Harcourt.

This tied the Morgan family with British aristocracy. The descendants of that family would include a chairman of Morgan Grenfell and Company, Lord William Harcourt.

Jack felt rather ashamed that he had so little contact with his father. Whenever Jack was asked whether or not Pierpont was going to attend the crowning of Edward VII, he would respond by saying that his father was a difficult man to keep tabs on, and that he had lost nearly all hope in trying to find him.

When Pierpont was going to a naval pageant in Spithead, Jack wanted to go along, but he said that his father "will probably not think of asking us." Pierpont did not really include Jack in the business, and he was kept in the dark regarding the business deals that were going on in his father's bank. To get information regarding the trusts of US Steel, he had to read the newspapers.

Although Pierpont loved his timid son, his son was not like him, and that bothered Pierpont. When he was young and even in his older days, Pierpont was ambitious, fiery, and aggressive. In contrast, Jack was timid, scared, and calm—too calm for Pierpont's liking. The fact that Pierpont did not include Jack in the business just made Jack feel worse. In 1899, Pierpont had been away from New York and was just departing from London. Jack told his mother by a letter about how things could not function when his father was not there. He went on to say, "I only hope it will never come to that with me.

Probably it won't, owing to the fact that things always will move on without me." This perhaps shows that Jack considered himself an unimportant player in the Morgan bank.

Pierpont's business was growing so large and the things he dealt with took up so much of his time and energy that he did not have room to deal with his timid, reserved, and insecure son. Jack was always standing in the shadows, waiting for his father to pick him up. He always waited for the day that his father would include him and have confidence in him.

Jack was much like his grandfather, Junius Spencer Morgan, in the way that he always kept an eye on the workload Pierpont was handling. He once saw Pierpont and his aunt, Mary Lyman, playing dominoes. He recounted the incident, "It is too funny to see Father and Aunt Mary gravely sitting down to play that imbecile game."

Jack also took care to account the regality and pride of his father. He said that after doing one good thing he felt absolutely proud. Aside from just seeing the funny and egotistic side of

Pierpont, though, Jack also saw in Pierpont what was behind the cold, brusque facade. He wrote, "He is very well and jolly by bits but sometimes I see he feels as lonely as I do and he looks as glum as if he hadn't a friend in the world."

Jack was taking care of both his parents. For his father, not directly, but was watching over him and giving both his father and mother his kindness. His mother, whose health was now faltering and somewhat deaf, was being cheered up by her son. Jack was not very happy about London but was much happier when his father said that he and his wife, Jessie, as she was known, could stay at Pierpont's 13 Princes Gate home. Pierpont soon took possession of the house next door, 14 Princes Gate, and the two residences joined together. 13 Princes Gate was filled with the artworks of Rembrandt, Rubens, Turner, and Velázquez, works of art that Pierpont had collected and spent a fortune on. Due to export duties, Pierpont never brought his vast art collection to the United States.

Aside from 13 Princes Gate, Jack also stayed in Dover House, the house that Junius had purchased. Jack was extremely happy that his father had been so kind and generous and had been more of a father to him in some time. He wrote to his mother, "He has been dear to us ever since we landed, most thoughtful of everything and immensely interested in Jessie's social career! I know he has much enjoyed our being in his house, for it must have been very lonely for him with no one there and we have not hampered him at all or bothered him with responsibilities."

By the time 1900 rolled around, the firm of J.P. Morgan and Company was one of the largest banks in the world. Pierpont focused on the reorganization and consolidation of companies. This sort of reorganization would come to be known as "morganization." One example of Pierpont's consolidation of companies was when he created the United States Steel Corporation, which included the steel company of steel tycoon Andrew Carnegie.

What was morganization? When several railroads in the United States were facing a financial crisis, the House of Morgan stepped in to save the day. Pierpont reorganized the railroad companies and placed them under his control. Most of the railroads east of the Mississippi River were nearly bankrupt and were morganized and placed under the control of the House of Morgan. The railroads that Pierpont morganized included the Lehigh Valley Railroad, the Chesapeake and Ohio, the Santa Fe, the Great Northern Railway, the Northern Pacific Railway, the New York Central, the Erie Railroad, the Southern Railway, the Philadelphia and Reading Railway Company, and the Jersey Central. Today, the Philadelphia and Reading Railway Company is called the Reading Company.

Although morganization placed the Morgan banking house at the helm of several railroad companies and furnished the Morgan partners with a great amount of money, it was dangerous work.

During the time of morganization, everyone worked late into the night. Everyone worked hard, and although the reward was wealth, the side effect was death. Some of the Morgan partners simply dropped dead. In one case, a certain Mr. Wood, one of the partners, who was waiting for the arrival of a train, dropped dead.

The trade-off was wealth for one's life.

Chapter 7 High Finance & Low Times

In 1879, the United States Congress established the gold standard, which, among other things, allowed holders of dollars to exchange their dollars for the equivalent value in gold. To make it look like more than an empty promise, the U.S. government made it a point to have a minimum of $100 million in gold in reserves.

The gold standard was greatly disliked by American farmers. Due to deflation, they could not sell their produce for high enough prices, but they had to repay their loans with a great deal of money. When inflation arrived, however, they could raise their prices.

The gold standard was a source of great consternation in the United States. Quite a few Western states made bankers illegal, and the state of Texas barred all bankers until 1904. Former Secretary of State and three-time Democratic presidential candidate William

Jennings Bryan riled up the Populists by speaking negatively about how the United States was financially dependent on Britain.

In 1893, a financial panic occurred, which resulted in a crisis for the gold standard. The federal gold reserve dipped below the minimum of $100 million. Because of the panic, overseas investors who had their money in American banks became worried and began to withdraw their money in gold, hastening the decrease of the gold reserve in the United States. In 1894, the gold reserve dropped to $68 million, and it seemed that the United States government might go bankrupt. Pierpont wanted to solve the problem and approached President Grover Cleveland. While Pierpont was waiting for an answer, he played solitaire.

Unfortunately, Cleveland did not want to meet Pierpont. He wanted to sell bonds to the public and get money from there. Congress, the branch of government that holds the purse, however, wouldn't allow it.

Pierpont understood that Cleveland's method was not going to work. The American government did not have enough time to sell enough bonds to fix everything it needed to. In the end, Pierpont traveled to Washington with Robert Bacon and Francis Lynde Stetson.

When Pierpont and his associates arrived in Washington, they were met by Daniel Lamont, the Secretary of War. Lamont told them that President Cleveland did not wish to meet them, and Pierpont replied in an authoritative tone saying that he was not going to leave until he met the president. In the end, Cleveland relented and decided to meet Pierpont.

The night before the meeting Pierpont played solitaire and then went to the White House the following morning. During the meeting with the president, he said very little and let the other attendees speak. He was in such distress at what he heard that his discomfort and unsettled state caused him to inadvertently crush his fist, which crushed his lit cigar in his palm. Crushed tobacco and amber fell on his trousers and the Oval Office floor.

In the midst of the conversation, Treasury Secretary John G. Carlisle received word that only $9 million was left in the federal gold reserves on Wall Street. Everyone was visibly restless at this point.

This is when Pierpont came in. He said he knew of a $10 million draft, but if they did not receive it, everything would be over by 3:00 p.m.

Presenting a demand draft against the United States Government and not getting paid for it would shatter the credit markets and plunge the U.S. economy overnight. The ensuing catastrophe would reverberate globally. The financial collapse would not be limited to North America but drag other economies with it. Everyone in the room was well aware of that fact.

The reticent Cleveland then turned to Pierpont for his opinion. Pierpont's plan was that his firm and that of the Rothschild's would purchase 3.5 million ounces worth of gold, of which at least half would come from Europe. In exchange for this gold, they would give $65 million in 30-year gold bonds.

His plan was financially and legally sound. An old piece of legislation enacted during the Civil War stipulated that the country could purchase gold from foreign countries. Pierpont used this to his advantage.

When Pierpont concluded, Cleveland quietly knew that Pierpont's proposal was the only solution. He presented Pierpont with a cigar from the humidor on his desk to replace the one Pierpont had crushed earlier. That cigar was a token of appreciation and a symbol of a truce between two men, who couldn't stand each other.

In the end, everything worked out well, and the gold reserves began to rise and stabilize. The draw on the reserves also diminished, and the dollar stabilized as well. Pierpont had solved the problem with an ingenious and workable solution.

On February 20, 1895, the bonds of the scheme were all sold in two hours in London and just twenty-two minutes in New York. Pierpont was delighted with the outcome. He remarked, "You cannot appreciate the relief to everybody's mind for the dangers were so great scarcely anyone dared whisper them." Although the scheme was a success, the parties involved in pulling it off were not looked on very favorably by most.

First of all, they had bought the bonds they would sell for the scheme for $104.25 each and made the first selling price of $112.25 for each of them. People were bidding on the price until it reached a sale price of $119. To some people, this was evidence that the people who had pulled off the scheme that for the time being saved the gold standard had practically been swindlers.

An interest rate of 3.75% was charged on the bonds, which was considered quite high. The bonds had been sold in just twenty-two minutes in New York as mentioned earlier, and several bankers were able to pocket up to $7 million, all of which was profit.

At a later date, Pierpont would argue that these amounts were exaggerated and were far from the real profits that were made. Pierpont went on to defend the group and said they had made less than 5 percent. Regardless of how much they made, the credibility of the United States had been saved, something that the naysayers to the transaction could neither understand nor appreciate.

Since the Rothschild family had been involved in the scheme, the condemnations and reproaches went further than just opposition to what the bankers had done. They were laced with a layer of anti-Semitism, for the Rothschilds were a Jewish banking house.

One man who opposed what the bankers had done to save the gold standard was William Jennings Bryan, who always said no to having any hints of anti-Semitism in his political fight with the banking houses that conducted the scheme.

When Bryan was running for president a year later, he once spoke to a number of Democrats in Chicago who were Jewish and said to them, "Our opponents have sometimes tried to make it appear that we are attacking a race when we denounced the financial policy of the Rothschilds. But we are not, we are as much opposed to the financial policy of J. Pierpont

Morgan as we are to the financial policy of the Rothschilds."

Despite what most thought, though, Pierpont saw his little plan as an act that turned out beautifully.

Pierpont's structure was, however, not a permanent fix. After all that hard work and public censure, the gold reserve in the United States Treasury once again began to dwindle.

When the time came for President Cleveland to fix the situation at the beginning of 1896, Pierpont came up with the idea of global collaboration to solve the problem. The group was meant to consist of Morgan, Harjes of Paris, the National City Bank of New York, and the Deutsche Bank of Berlin.

Unfortunately for Pierpont, however, President Cleveland was not interested in causing an uproar among the Populists again and wanted to proceed with a loan. Because of this, Pierpont only made half of the bond issue, which amounted to $67 million.

For his firm and all bankers alike, if governments stayed weak and ran on tight budgets, then Pierpont and his fellow bankers would all gain. President Cleveland was not upset with the popular reaction to Pierpont's scheme and heartily praised Pierpont for what he did, saying that Pierpont was a patriot.

Because of Cleveland's attitude toward Pierpont, he lost several supporters, and during the presidential elections in 1896, William Jennings Bryan was more popular than Cleveland.

William Jennings Bryan opposed large businesses, such as the companies of oil magnate John D. Rockefeller and the steel company of Andrew Carnegie. People like J.P. Morgan would also have trouble with Bryan because he was going after large corporations, which included Pierpont's firm.

William Jennings Bryan was going to tear down these large firms if he became president, and no industrial tycoon or Pierpont wanted that to happen.

At the time, such magnates as Andrew Carnegie and John D. Rockefeller were making substantial profits, but the workers in their steel plants and oil refineries were in poor condition. Workers would die while working in the steel plants, and others survived to feel the pain of hard work. Most were earning less than a dollar a day. They were all poor, and Bryan's message, however misguided, resonated with them. He managed to vilify the titans who were responsible for building America.

During the 1896 election, people wanted better for themselves, and they wanted Bryan to be president. The titans of industry, however, wanted Bryan as far away from the White House as possible, for with him as president, their businesses would face tremendous headwinds. J.P. Morgan also wanted Bryan out of the White House. Pierpont's ever-expanding firm was always growing larger, and its growth and dominance would be broken by a man like Bryan.

To save their businesses and everything they built, Rockefeller, Carnegie, and J.P. Morgan teamed up to defeat William Jennings Bryan by supporting his opponent in the general election.

To do this, they donated heavily to Republican William McKinley's campaign. McKinley supported big businesses and would allow Pierpont and the others to proceed unchecked. Each of them donated more $200,000 to McKinley's campaign (more than $6 million today).

That battle at the ballot box was one of consequence. Pursuant to the structure that Pierpont had envisioned and executed to save the gold standard, the battle between McKinley and Bryan was about exactly that. The departure from the gold standard to one that was bi-metallic. McKinley advocated remaining on the gold standard, but Bryan was going after the popular vote of the everyday worker. He used his oratory skills to rile up the base and cast dispersion at the titans of industry. They fell for it. Even with McKinley's better proposals, his win wasn't as decisive as he had hoped.

In 1896, William McKinley became President of the United States. With a man who supported large corporations now leading the country, Carnegie and Rockefeller could go on advancing their business without any hindrances. Pierpont could also continue to expand his business and advance his bank without any problems.

Train Trouble

In the late 1800s, the railroad industry was suffering from rate wars and problems between different railroad companies. The most important of these problems were between the Pennsylvania Railroad Company and the New York Central Railroad of Cornelius Vanderbilt. The issue at hand was the West Shoreline, a small railway that was being built parallel to the New York Central Railroad on the Hudson River, although it was running on the opposite bank. Railroads such as these were being created by people who simply understood how the railroad business worked. Railroads were very easily put in danger when competition entered the picture.

This was a time when people were building rival railroads just so they could later sell them to the big railroad companies. They were thus able to make a nice profit in the end.

It was believed that the Pennsylvania Railroad Company was the one behind the West Shoreline, and thus the New York Central locked horns with it. It began to build a line parallel to a Pennsylvania railroad. The fight between the two companies was a never-ending war that would have led to the collapse of both companies had it not been for John Pierpont Morgan.

Seeing that things needed to be fixed, he got the presidents of the two companies to meet aboard his yacht, the *Corsair*. At first, the men did nothing, and the *Corsair* simply sailed up and down the Hudson River. It soon became obvious that Pierpont wasn't going to let them off his yacht until they had come to an agreement. In the end, a compromise was reached, which became known as the Corsair Compact. The New York Central would incorporate the West Shoreline into their railway, having a second railroad running along the Hudson River.

Steep Merger

In 1901, Pierpont would consolidate several manufacturing companies to form the United States Steel Corporation, which used to be the largest producer of steel. Pierpont wanted to include Carnegie Steel Company in the corporation, but to so, he needed to purchase it. He began negotiations with the president of Carnegie Steel, Charles M. Schwab. Eventually, Carnegie would write down on a piece of paper the price at which he was willing to sell his company: $480 million. A moment after Pierpont was shown the price he said yes.

This payment was the largest transaction that has ever been made in the history of the modern world. That $480 million is equivalent to more than $14.2 billion today.

Carnegie was happy, but he later realized that he had actually sold his company too cheap—almost by $100 million, and that is why Pierpont agreed to the price with such speed. When he admitted this fact to Pierpont, Pierpont simply said, "Very likely, Andrew."

As for the relationship between Pierpont and Carnegie, Carnegie liked Pierpont's father, Junius, but not Pierpont. Pierpont, on the other hand, found people like Carnegie too gruff for his standards. The pair mixed like oil and water. They never really could get along.

For his part, Carnegie did not like Pierpont for his extramarital affairs. As the president of Carnegie Steel and later the first president of US Steel and cofounder of Bethlehem Steel, Mr. Charles Schwab said of Carnegie, "Carnegie frowned on anything savoring of the flesh and the devil."

Aside from just including many other companies and that of Carnegie Steel, it also included the companies of William Henry "Judge" Moore and Elbert Gary, the second president of US Steel. William Henry Moore was both a financier and a lawyer. He was a director of a number of steel manufacturing concerns that were part of the amalgamation that was US Steel. His brother, James Hobart Moore, and himself had a role in founding the First National Bank, the American Can Company, the National Biscuit Company, the Diamond Match Company, the Delaware, Lackawanna and Western Railroad, the Lehigh Valley Railroad, the Continental Fire Insurance Company, the American Cotton Oil Company, the Chicago, Rock Island and Pacific Railroad, the Western Union Telegraph Company, and Bankers Trust.

The United States Steel Corporation took up its headquarters in the Empire Building at 71 Broadway on Manhattan Island. They would have their headquarters here for seventy-five years.

With Carnegie Steel now in his possession, Pierpont could go on to form US Steel. Before he bought Carnegie Steel, Pierpont financed a company called Federal Steel Company. He combined Federal Steel, Carnegie Steel Company, American Tin Plate, Shelby Steel Tube, American Steel Hoop, American Sheet Steel, Wire Company, Consolidated Steel, and National Tube. Wire Company and Consolidated Steel belonged to the philanthropist, businessman, and inventor William Edenborn. Shortly after the formation of US Steel in 1901, two other companies were incorporated into the trust: Lake Superior Consolidated Mines and American Bridge. Lake Superior Consolidated Mines was in the control of Standard Oil founder John D. Rockefeller.

Many other industrial companies would be included in the trust in the years to come.

This new trust that was the US Steel Corporation was seen by some as a company that was acting as a monopoly in several kinds of industries. In reality, the company was trying to do it all. It was attempting to make railroad cars as well as rails, nails, wire, bridges, and even ships, so it's understandable why other people saw it as a monopoly.

US Steel was the first billion dollar company to ever exist, at one time being worth $1.4 billion, which is about $41 billion today. Although $41 billion really isn't much today, a company being worth more than $1 billion in 1901 was both unprecedented and mind-boggling.

Schwab and others believed that because it was so large US Steel would be able to advance and become even better. When US Steel was first created, the company had a lot of business, and it was predicted that it would eventually produce 75 percent of all the steel produced in the United States. In 1902, it came close. That year it produced 67 percent of the steel in the country.

Business contracted for US Steel at the end of 1901, and with the prosperity of US Steel retracing, Charles Schwab struck out on his own to create the largest steel producing company second to US Steel, which was Bethlehem Steel, founded in 1904. He partnered with Joseph Wharton to start Bethlehem Steel, which eventually became America's largest shipbuilding concern at one point in its history.

Railroad Consolidation

The year that Pierpont bought Carnegie Steel he also founded the Northern Securities Company along with James J. Hill and Edward Henry Harriman. The Northern Securities Company was the amalgamation of the Chicago, Burlington and Quincy Railroad, the North Pacific Railway, and the Great Northern

Railway, which was founded by James J. Hill in 1889.

James J. Hill was president of the Great Northern Railway and a minority shareholder of the Northern Pacific Railway. Edward Harriman controlled the Union Pacific Railroad, one of the largest railroad companies in the nation. Both the Union Pacific and the Great Northern Railroad wanted dominance over the Chicago, Burlington and Quincy Railroad to join their own railroads to be the focal point of railways in Chicago. In the end, Hill managed to win over the CB&Q Railroad by buying the shares of the company for $200 each.

When the Northern Pacific Railroad owned up to 40 percent of the stock of CB&Q Railroad, Harriman began a stock raid aimed at the Northern Pacific Railroad.

If Harriman controlled the Northern Pacific, he would be able to decide who were the directors of the board of the CB&Q Railroad. This would place the Union Pacific Railroad, which was under Harriman, in a better position. The stock raid Harriman began against the Northern

Pacific Railroad caused the first stock market crash afecting the NYSE (New York Stock Exchange.) In the end, it would be resolved by formation of the Northern Securities Company, a trust that wouldn't last for long.

Investors had previously sold shares that were not theirs to sell and were now eager to buy up shares regardless of the price. It is believed that some of the shares were sold for as much as $1,000. In the end, thanks to Pierpont Morgan, Hill was able to assume a majority shareholder's position in the Northern Pacific Railroad in spite of what Harriman had done to prevent it.

The Northern Securities Company served Hill as a way to control the stock of his vast railroad empire. Several directors who worked for Harriman became representatives of some of the holdings that Hill had regarding shares of the Northern Pacific Railroad.

The Northern Securities Company was the combination of the Northern Pacific Railroad, the Great Northern Railroad, and the Union Pacific Railroad. Pierpont believed that merging these companies would bring peace to the railroad business and be a better alternative. Others, however, saw the Northern Securities Company as yet another way that Pierpont was gaining more power.

Chapter 8 Turning Tides

In 1900, William McKinley was reelected and began his second term in the White House in March 1901. It seemed that big business was still safe. It was during this time that Theodore Roosevelt entered the picture.

Roosevelt was from a wealthy family and chose to have a career in politics. The problem, however, was his public appearance. He was a rich kid. He thus set out to change his appearance and took photographs holding hunting rifles and made himself look less aristocratic. He then enlisted in the army and served in the Spanish-American War. After that, Roosevelt no longer appeared as a rich kid but a daring warrior who had served his country. At the end of the war, he entered politics.

Unlike McKinley, he was greatly opposed to big business and multicorporation companies. His views were antithetical to Pierpont and the other tycoons of industry.

Six months into McKinley's second term, an out-of-work factory hand by the name of Leon Czolgosz assassinated him—no doubt riled up by the rhetoric of William Jennings Bryan.

President McKinley was at the Pan-American Exhibition in Buffalo when Leon Czolgosz shot him twice. Czolgosz was tried and found guilty, and sentenced to death. He was executed on October 29, 1901, approximately forty-six days after he shot William McKinley, and approximately thirty-eight days after McKinley passed away on September 14, 1901.

With McKinley gone and the nation in shock, Pierpont and Rockefeller were now facing an enemy they were not expecting. They had engineered that Roosevelt would replace McKinley.

With McKinley gone, Theodore Roosevelt ascended to the presidency, and Pierpont's business was immediately in trouble. Roosevelt set out to tear down Northern Securities Company in the name of competition and monopoly.

Near the end of February 1902, the U.S. Department of Justice declared that it was filing a lawsuit against Northern Securities. It was going after Pierpont's corporation under orders from President Theodore Roosevelt. They were attacking the company on the basis of violating the Sherman Antitrust Act, which was created twelve years earlier in 1890. The case, known as Northern Securities Co. v. United States, was one of the first antitrust cases. It went all the way to the Supreme Court and lost five to four.

Over the next seven years, other trusts would fall victim to antitrust policies. U.S. government cases against trusts would cause their dismantling. One such case was when the railroad empire of Edward Henry Harriman, which included both the Southern Pacific and the Union Pacific Railroad, was broken.

Pierpont was incensed over the breakup of Northern Securities. He did not like politicians or anyone for that matter to tell him how to run *his* business. Unfortunately for Pierpont, however, the government won. In 1904, the Northern Securities Company was dissolved, and the three railroads that had merged to form the company were on their own again.

In 1955, fifty-one years after the dissolution of the Northern Securities Company, the Great Northern Railroad and the Northern Pacific Railroad revisited the issue of uniting. In the end, everything was a success. The United States Supreme Court gave its approval of the merger and on March 2, 1970, the Chicago, Burlington and Quincy Railroad, The Great Northern Railroad, the Spokane, Portland and Seattle Railway, and the Northern Pacific Railroad consolidated to form the Burlington Northern Railroad. It would later be turned into the Burlington Northern Santa Fe Railway or BSNF Railway.

Although Pierpont had lost to the U.S. government, this did not mean that he stopped increasing his power.

When Panama became independent thanks to Theodore Roosevelt, Pierpont's firm became the country's fiscal agent. Instead of seething at Roosevelt in perpetuity, he helped with building the Panama Canal.

Chapter 9 The Panama Canal

The United States wanted to gain control of the Panama Canal and the shipping traffic that passes through it. The well-to-do inhabitants of Panama understood that they were better off working for the benefit of the Americans than remaining a poor South American country.

The Panama Canal is a forty-eight mile passage through the Isthmus of Panama constructed for ships to pass through from the Atlantic to the Pacific. The Panama Canal is approximately forty feet deep and has a minimum width at the bottom of five hundred feet. Construction began near the end of 1903 and was completed approximately eleven years later in 1914. Seventy-five thousand workers constructed the canal, and 5,609 of them died while it was being built either from sickness or accidents. Of those 5,609, 4,500 were West Indians.

Construction cost $375 million. This figure includes $40 million the United States paid to France and the $10 million paid to Panama.

Both payments were handled by J.P. Morgan and Company.

Construction of the Panama Canal was the most expensive building project ever taken on by the United States at the time.

The chief engineers included John Findlay Wallace, John Frank Stevens, and George Washington Goethals.

Fifteen days after Panama gained its independence from Colombia, the United States of America and the newly created Panama signed the Hay-Bunau-Varilla Treaty, which designated the Panama Canal Zone and laid the foundation for construction of the Panama Canal.

It was around this time that Colombia was entangled in what is known as the Thousand Day War. It began in 1899 and ended in 1902. It was a war between the Liberal Party of Colombia, the Conservative Party, and radical groups in the country. Panama was one of the places in which this conflict was fought.

The United States government was going to pay $40 million to the New Panama Canal Company of France, or the Compagnie Nouvelle du Canal de Panamá. This money was meant to gain the rights to use the resources belonging to the company and also gain permission to build the Panama Canal, which would cut through the isthmus.

The $10 milliom paid to Panama was meant to secure the land for the Panama Canal forever. Furthermore, in accordance with the Hay-Bunau-Varilla Treaty, the United States was to pay $250,000 every year as a rental fee.

Pierpont's firm was chosen by the Treasury Secretary of the United States, Leslie Mortier Shaw, to manage the transaction with the French.

Pierpont headed several American banks into slowly turning the Republic of Panama into a tax haven, which eventually became a money laundering haven.

In the beginning, the Republic of Panama got ships from other countries to transport Standard

Oil goods to not have to pay taxes to the United States.

The Panama Canal gave the United States control of both the Atlantic and the Pacific Ocean. Thanks to the Panama Canal, ships did not have to travel down to the southern tip of South America and then come back up. If you were living in San Francisco and wanted to travel by ship to New York, you would have had to travel south to hazardous waters south of South America and turn back up. After the construction of the Panama Canal, you could sail just a little south, cut through Central America by way of the canal, and then go up to New York. It saved most ships traveling from the Pacific to the Atlantic a great deal of time and money. It also reduced the risk of disaster.

Sadly, Pierpont was not able to see the first ship that passed through the Panama Canal on August 15, 1914. He had financed the canal, and it was a great success, yet he wasn't able to see it work.

It was a totally American endeavor, from the electricity generation invented by Thomas Alva

Edison, the finance and structure by J.P. Morgan, and the oil of John D. Rockefeller to run the generators and motors to make the canal function properly.

Chapter 10 Humble Pie

Several years after construction was started on the Panama Canal, a financial panic gripped the country in 1907, and Roosevelt was forced to call on the man he had persecuted in the Northern Securities antitrust case. Pierpont had already proved himself, and there was no one Roosevelt could turn to but him.

From 1906 to 1907, everyone knew there was an impending financial crisis. One thing in international finance that you can't have is the rumor of impending doom because that rumor almost always feeds on itself and becomes a self-fulfilling prophecy. Once the rumor was on the street, depositors began withdrawing their savings. Since a bank lives on deposits, there was a run on banks, and the delicate balance of finance started to destabilize.

When depositors withdraw, banks need to find cash to satisfy the withdrawals, and they typically do this in one of two ways. They either call back loans they have made, or they liquidate their investments.

That has a ripple effect. Liquidating investments has an added effect. To liquidate their investments means they would have to dump stocks or bonds that they had invested in, which has a further impact. The stock market would fall. This is what happened in 1907.

Everyone was hastily withdrawing their money from banks, and there was so much selling on the New York Stock Exchange that it soon crashed. As the funds got sucked out of the system, the credit markets came to a halt.

While all this was going on, Pierpont was out of the scene and enjoying church activities. He transported bishops on private railway cars and was busy attending the Episcopal Convention in Richmond, Virginia. Pierpont also had with him a relative of his personal physician, Dr. James Markoe. She was from California, and her name was Mrs. John Markoe. She has sometimes been suspected of having been a mistress of Pierpont.

Back in New York, luminaries in the corporate world, such as William Rockefeller, Edward Henry Harriman, Jacob Schiff, and Henry Clay Frick, came together and held a secret meeting at the Corner.

They came up with a plan, but when Pierpont heard about it he said it was foolish, and the plan was canceled the following day.

During the time when Pierpont was traveling through Europe on his yacht, the partners of the Morgan bank were constantly warning him that something bad was going to happen at the stock exchange.

On the day of the panic, Pierpont was attending the Episcopal Convention in Richmond. Gradually, more and more cables from Pierpont's office on Wall Street began to arrive in the middle of the convention. Each cable was more pressing than the last. Pierpont, knowing that something was wrong, although clueless as to what to do, headed back to his office on Wall Street. In a humbling reversal of demeanor, Teddy Roosevelt had to approach J.P. Morgan to help steer the country out of the Crash of 1907.

There was no love lost between the two men, especially since it was Roosevelt's Justice Department that broke up Northern Securities. What happened next was nothing short of a miracle.

Chapter 11 Crash of 1907

Market crashes are not a trivial matter to be trifled with. Sovereign governments go to great lengths to avoid them, but in this case, they had inadvertently caused it. Now they needed help to fix it. The agency that would be in the driver's seat if a crash occurred today would be the Federal Reserve, but in 1907 it was yet to be legislated into existence.

ECON 101

Modern economies work when a number of factors come together. There must be activated, which is measured by GDP and growth. When a country is producing output, regardless of what that output is, whether industrial, agricultural, or technological, the output creates the basis of the economy. The second factor is the liquidity of the system that allows the movement of funds to be directed where they need to go to reward the factors of output, act as consideration for the infrastructure that supports that output, and allows for the expansion of that system. Liquidity is defined by money supply and demand. The greater the demand with reduced supply results in an illiquid economy and recessionary forces; conversely, the greater the supply of money and reduced demand results in inflationary forces. Either side of the spectrum is not ideal. Governments have numerous tools at their disposal to adjust the balance between recessionary and inflationary forces. Finally, an economy needs external activity. In most cases, that comes in the form of trade with other economies. Without the other economies to consume the output of this country, there will be no injection of new liquidity into the system, and thus there will be diminished growth. The only growth that results from an economy that has no new demand will be inflationary in nature.

Within the context of these three factors, it is easier to define the anatomy of a market crash. There are two sides to every stock market. The stock market acts as a barometer for the overall economy from the perspective of the demand for the stocks as an investment avenue for excess capital on one hand. On the other, it acts as a measure for the future valuation of potential. In other words, it values the growth potential of the output factors.

When there are excess funds in the system, instead of it sitting idly, bankers put it to good use by buying us stock from the stock market. That increased demand nudges the process higher, and those higher prices appear as a lofty stock market—something we have taken, albeit erroneously, to mean a healthy economy. When there is insufficient liquidity in the money supply of the capital markets in general, then the value of investment-grade assets are disposed of to convert their holdings to cash or liquid assets. That disposal of investment assets sends their prices falling.

The third element in an economy is the confidence of its participants. Consumer confidence is key in determining everything from discretionary spending to savings levels. On one end of that spectrum is how much people tend to save. The more they save, the more banks have an excess supply of funds. They take that excess supply and invest it in a number of avenues. Banks can lend it out to others who are planning expansion in the next economic cycle. They could invest in the stock market, which will see the process rise. But what happens when consumers are so worried about their money that they do not spend it and do not want to leave it in the bank? They withdraw it and put it under their pillow. Then all that liquidity is sucked out of the system, and there is no money to do anything in the economy. It is like the kid who takes his ball home—everyone can't play. In the same way, the consumer and saver become worried about the economy because of a poor outlook, political uncertainty, or just a bad rumor.

In a typical stock market crash, one of the factors fails, and that precipitates a crash. It could be that the output of the country comes to a halt. If there is no output, there is no creation of goods and services, which results in zero rewards and zero value. Without value there is no basis for the value of a stock, and that completely erodes the wealth that is locked in the value of a stock and thus the stock market. Or the liquidity of the capital markets could diminish, and that creates a scenario where there is no capital to move from one sector of the economy (let's say the savings side of the equation) to the investing side of the equation. Capital flows stop, and the economy comes to a halt. Or, the third is that the confidence of what could happen in the future results in a withdrawal from the system, and that deflates the air out of the system, which results in a crashed economy.

Overview of the Crash

In the case of the Crash of 1907, it was a combination of many factors. The first was the overzealousness of Roosevelt's trust-busting. That just set the scene. There were, however, three vitiating events that created the perfect storm.

First, a failed attempt at manipulating the stock price of the United Copper Company by the Heinze brothers resulted in the stock market plunging. That, in turn, caused a rumor that the third-largest banking trust in New York, Knickerbocker Trust, was somehow involved in the scheme to manipulate the stock price, and that they may be in trouble with trust-busting Roosevelt. That unsubstantiated rumor caused a run on Knickerbocker within a week of the failed stock manipulation. Within a span of three hours, on October 22, $8 million (equivalent to $250 million in today's value) was withdrawn by more than 15,000 depositors who lined up around the block. This created a liquidity crisis. Knickerbocker ran out of cash to pay depositors. That is one of the reasons why the Crash of 1907 is called the Knickerbocker Crisis.

Without any liquidity, the third-largest bank had to stop trading on the stock exchange and liquidate many of their other holdings to be able to cover their obligations. That created a further drop in the market.

On October 21, a Monday, copper shares dropped dramatically, which weakened the trusts in New York. That created a further liquidation of shares on the stock exchange to cover losses on the copper market.

Within two days, on October 24, a further two dozen trading houses across the country had been sucked into the downward spiral and had stopped trading.

News of these events and the corresponding price drops and volume of trades were part of the messages Pierpont was receiving with increasing frequency as he attended the Episcopal Convention.

At first, he was not inclined to get involved. His frustrations with Roosevelt were certainly a factor, but after Roosevelt requested his help, it dawned on him that it was more about the country than the frustrations between them.

After returning to New York, Pierpont analyzed the problem and understood the factors and nuances of the predicament. He understood that the key to unwinding the situation was to restore confidence in the system and do what would require the infusion of capital to buoy the credit and stock markets.

As soon as he got back, he convened a meeting with many of the principals involved on both sides of the equation. They were from companies that were not affected as well as from those that were already underwater. His first act was to stop the hemorrhage.

He also contacted such men as Rockefeller to lend their liquidity to hold the markets from descending further. They obliged. The plan began to work. The stock market that had lost 50 percent of its value before Pierpont's involvement had now stopped its descent, and while it didn't get back up to pre-crash levels, it had at least regained the markets' collective confidence. A sigh of relief could be heard from Wall Street to Main Street.

Two weeks after Pierpont began work fixing everything up, he had already provided enough liquidity to the system that allowed it to do a course correction and return to a stable version of itself. Men like Rockefeller and others who had lent their liquidity to the system were able to reap modest profits in a matter of weeks, and companies that would have otherwise failed were rescued from the brink. Pierpont's plan had saved many trust organizations, trading houses, banking houses, and the New York Stock Exchange.

The cause of the 1907 panic had been attributed to several things. One was President Theodore Roosevelt's speech in which he inveighed against the wealthy men of the country. In his zeal to shore up populist support, he had neglected and underestimated the contribution to stability that the same men of society he was targeting were the ones keeping the economy together.

Another area that contributed to all this was a tight money supply that was inadvertently in effect. The money supply tools that the government has today were not available at the turn of the century.

In the post mortem to the crash, another element that Pierpont realized was that banks had made numerous loans based on the collateral of stock. There was also a very liberal policy in doing so. Would-be investors would seek a loan, perhaps one-fifth of the price of the stock. In essence, today we call that buying on margin. What happens when the price of the stock falls in excess of the margin? The bank is required to liquidate the stock if the borrower can't come up with the funds to cover the adverse price movement. This is also what happened widely across the trading houses. It is one of the reasons the ripples started touching the two dozen trading houses across the country.

One of the things that Morgan had to do was instruct the trading houses to not liquidate the stocks and then inject the liquidity so that they could hold onto those counters while the market rebounded and unlocked the margin call. It was a severe case of Catch-22, but the force of Pierpont's personality convinced them to do it and placed the resource of cash to help them do it.

Sometime earlier two bankers by the name of Thomas William Lamont Jr. and Henry Pomeroy Davison had set up a new mechanism known as Bankers Trust, which was a company whose founding was aided by William Henry Moore as mentioned before. Lamont was the man who asked in 1946 for the letter Queen Victoria had written in "honor" of Peabody.

Lamont was from Liberty Bank, and Pomeroy was from the First National Bank.

Bankers Trust was a firm that would own trusts. After all, commercial banks were not allowed to conduct business regarding trusts, but they could own them. Pierpont would hand over people who were in the business of trusts to Bankers Trust, and after the BT was done with them, they would be directed back to Pierpont's firm.

When Pierpont needed to lend liquidity to the system in the wake of the 1907 Crash, he put together a syndicate of bankers. Among this committee were Benjamin Strong from Bankers Trust and Henry Pomeroy Davison from the First National Bank. This group of bankers was told to go in and verify the books at Knickerbocker. Later, when Benjamin Strong was the governor of the Federal Reserve Bank in New York, he would tell of how he once saw the sad and anxious faces of the people who had deposited money at Knickerbocker Trust. He said, "The consternation of the faces of the people in the line, many of them I knew, I shall never forget. I know that Harry left the building with a sense of dejection and deafest, which it is quite impossible for me to describe."

How it Went Down

Pierpont deemed that Knickerbocker Trust was bound to fail. On October 22, the day that people were lining up to withdraw their money, Knickerbocker Trust collapsed.

Several weeks later, when the former president of Knickerbocker Trust wanted to meet with Pierpont, he was not allowed to. He then committed suicide by shooting himself. His suicide caused a wave of suicides among people who had placed their money in the trust.

On one Tuesday night, Pierpont held a meeting with several other bankers as well as the Treasury Secretary, George B. Cortelyou, in a hotel in New York. Cortelyou promised that the government and the bankers would work together. The following day Cortelyou gave Pierpont $25 million of government money to fix the situation.

This was under orders from President Roosevelt.

The collapse of Knickerbocker Trust caused runs to take place at other trusts, mainly the Trust Company of America, which was not very far from Pierpont's office. On October 23 Pierpont held a meeting of the presidents of the different trusts and tried to make them join up and become a force that would fix everything.

Unfortunately, however, they were not able to work together very well because they did not know each other. After Benjamin Strong of Bankers Trust revealed that everything was good with the Trust Company of America, Pierpont, in his greatly authoritative tone, said, "This is the place to stop the trouble, then." The Trust Company of America was obviously not doing well at the time due to the panic, but the report given by Strong simply showed that they were a firm worth saving.

George Fisher Baker, cofounder of the First National Bank; James Jewett Stillman, chairman of the National City Bank; and Pierpont put together $3 million to rescue the Trust Company of America.

During the two weeks that Pierpont was fixing the crash, people constantly withdrew their money from banks. People would set up seating areas and bring provisions and wait through the night for their bank to open so that they could rush in and withdraw their money. New York police gave people numbers to hold their places in line. A certain Sidney Weinberg, who would later be part of the largest bank in the world, Goldman Sachs, was being paid $10 a day to hold people's places.

At the time, the technique that was used to prevent banks from closing down and reducing the number of withdrawals was for the tellers of the bank to count the money very slowly. Annoying but effective.

The trusts of New York were now devoid of fiat currency to give to people who were withdrawing their money. So, the margin loans they had loaned were called back. Those shares that people had bought with the margin loans were then sold, and the money made from selling those shares was used by the trusts to give money to the people who were withdrawing their money from them. The bad thing about this, however, was that when the trusts were calling back their margin loans and people were selling their shares, the stock price of those shares dropped even further, worsening the panic. Although the trusts were calling back their margin loans, they continued to not have enough money to give their customers who were frantically withdrawing their deposits.

Even during the crisis, the trusts continued to give margin loans but at an exorbitant interest rate of 150 percent!

George Walbridge Perkins, Pierpont's right-hand man, sent a telegram to Jack, who was at the time in London, describing the chaos at Wall Street. He wrote, "At all times during the day there were frantic men and women in our offices, in every way giving evidence of the tremendous strain they were under."

All day long Pierpont was constantly bombarded by brokers who were about to be financially destroyed and needed aid. The Corner was filled with nervous men.

Pierpont was the only man who was calm and could fix everything. All the worried people on Wall Street flocked to the doors of 23 Wall Street and were looking up at the windows of the building as they approached.

On October 24, all trading of stocks had virtually stopped. Ransom H. Thomas, former president of the New York Stock Exchange, met with Pierpont and told him that fifty brokerage firms had the possibility of collapse if $25 million could not be put together that instant. He also wanted to close the NYSE for the time being. Pierpont then asked him, "At what time do you usually close it?" In truth, the NYSE was only a short walk away from Pierpont's office. What's funny is that he didn't know the schedule of the New York Stock Exchange.

Thomas replied, "Why, at 3:00." Pierpont wagged his finger and said that the New York Stock Exchange was not to close until that time.

At 2:00, Pierpont convened a meeting of several presidents of prominent New York banking firms and told them that unless $25 million was put together within the next dozen minutes, a great many brokerage firms were going to collapse. Approximately sixteen minutes later, it was agreed that the money would be given.

After that was settled, Pierpont sent a group of people to go to the Stock Exchange and tell everyone that margin loans were obtainable, and that their interest rate was a mere 10 percent.

A Mr. Amory Hodges, one of the people who had been charged with the duty of telling everyone about the margin loans, had his waistcoat ripped off while men rushed and bumped him frantically. That was the degree of chaos that reigned on Wall Street during the panic. Men were tearing up and down shouting and bumping into one another.

After the announcement was made, everyone cheered, and Pierpont, who was on the other side of Wall Street, heard the noise. He asked what the noise was about. What was happening was that the traders of the Stock Exchange were cheering for him.

On October 25, interest rates on margin loans skyrocketed once more. That week alone eight trusts and banking firms collapsed. Pierpont went to the New York Clearing House that day, which is where checks were cleared. He told the Clearing House to send out scripts to act as a backup form of money because of the dangerously low amount of green money.

Pierpont was very determined as he walked to the Clearing House. It seemed as if he didn't see the masses at Wall Street. He walked with his hat perched firmly on his head, his half-smoked cigar in his mouth, a piece of paper held firmly in his hand. As he walked, people in his path moved out of his way, but others who continued to stand there were pushed out of the way by Pierpont.

What differentiated him from everyone else, according to Pierpont's son-in-law, Herbert L. Satterlee, was that he was always steady in his walk. The other men around him ran here and there and generally walked in an unsteady fashion. In contrast, Pierpont walked calmly, determinedly, and steadily.

On the evening of the following day, October 26, Pierpont spoke to several religious leaders in

New York and told them to talk about being calm in their sermons. On Sunday morning, a certain archbishop by the name of Mr. Farley gave a sermon meant for businessmen.

By this time, Pierpont had been suffering from a violent cold for some time and headed to his Cragston home to spend the weekend. On October 28, a Monday, the mayor of New York City, George B. McClellan, went to the Morgan Library with a problem. Foreign investors in Europe were withdrawing their money from the United States. According to McClellan, New York needed $30 million to settle everything. In the end, George Baker of the First National Bank, Pierpont, and James Stillman of the National City Bank took up the job of putting together the money.

Pierpont ordered that a group of bankers were to keep on eye on how all the firms in the city were keeping their books.

Pierpont was now seventy years old and suffering from a violent cold at the time, yet he was able to handle the crisis of 1907 well and easily. He did not stop working despite his cold and spent nineteen-hour days working as he sucked on throat lozenges.

During his time fixing up the 1907 panic, Pierpont said that he missed Jack. Although he did not really have much confidence in him, Pierpont still loved his son.

Once in a while Pierpont's personal physician, Dr. James Markoe, gave him all sorts of gargles and sprays to soothe his illness. Dr. Markoe also told Pierpont that he should reduce his smoking to a maximum of twenty cigars a day. That should show you that he actually smoked a lot on a regular basis.

During extremely important meetings, the titan banker and the king of finance would sometimes fall asleep, and no one wanted to disturb him. One of the bankers at the meeting once gently removed the cigar in Pierpont's hands that was damaging the varnish on the table as he slept.

Pierpont would fall asleep at meetings for half an hour, while the other attendees talked about loans.

On November 2, Pierpont came up with a plan to save the Lincoln Trust, the Trust Company of America, and a brokerage firm known as Moore and Schley, which owned a large amount of Tennessee Coal, Iron, and Railroad shares that it was using as collateral for its loans. It also had a lot of debt.

Pierpont then convened a meeting of several bankers of New York and held the meeting at his private library, known today as the Pierpont Morgan Library.

US Steel Benefits from the Crash

Pierpont wanted something in return for his troubles.

He was, after all, the quintessential banker, and he didn't see anything wrong in making money out of this calamity while helping his country stave off ruin.

Pierpont's plan was to purchase the TCI shares of Moore and Schley. This would be helpful to the United States Steel Corporation, for the Tennessee Coal, Iron and Railroad Company was a competitor of US Steel and owned several well-to-do mines. Pierpont understood that with TCI tied to him US Steel would be able to make nice profits from TCI's iron ore and coal sites located in Alabama, Tennessee, and Georgia.

It was difficult to achieve this, however, due to antitrust policies and a president who tore down trusts and went after "monopolies."

What Pierpont did was say that he would purchase the TCI shares from Moore and Schley only if the bankers that had met in his library put together $25 million that would be used to save the weaker trust companies.

When Pierpont left to let the men discuss the issue, he closed the door behind him, locked it, and took the key with him. He then played solitaire that night in a room nearby. Sometimes, his staff would come in and tell him that the trust presidents in the locked room had come up with a proposition, and Pierpont would say it wasn't enough and would continue playing his game.

At 4:45 the following morning, Pierpont entered the room where the exhausted bankers had not reached a decision. He placed a gold pen in Edward King's hand, the man who led the trust presidents who were there. Pierpont then said, "Here's the place, King, and here's the pen." Tired out from their long night, King signed the paper, and the other presidents did so as well. Everyone then agreed to set aside $25 million for the purpose of saving the weaker trusts.

That night Elbert Gary, who was at the time president of US Steel, and Henry Clay Frick traveled to Washington. They were going there to get Roosevelt's green light for Pierpont's plans. They needed his approval before the stock market opened the following morning at 10:00.

They met with Roosevelt while he was still eating breakfast. Roosevelt did not object to their plans and gave them his approval. In essence, what happened was that Roosevelt agreed not to attack US Steel for Sherman Antitrust Act violations if they purchased the TCI shares. He understood the dire situation that existed and did not cause any problems.

From the White House, Elbert Gary telephoned Perkins, who was at Wall Street, at 9:55 and told him they had been given Roosevelt's approval.

The stock market was thrown into a frenzy. People suspected that Pierpont had swindled Roosevelt into not attacking him with issues of antitrust. Senator Robert La Follette of the state of Wisconsin said that the banking firms of Wall Street instigated the 1907 panic so that they could make a nice profit from it.

In the end, Pierpont purchased the TCI shares from Moore and Schley for $45 million.

Later, Grant B. Schley, partner of John G. Moore and cofounder of Moore and Schley, said that he could have simply borrowed the money to pay off the firm's debt instead of liquidating the firm's shares of TCI. In the end, the entire operation benefited Pierpont and US Steel. US Steel had less of a competitor, which was beneficial to Pierpont. So, Pierpont not only saved the country but also got something for himself and his trust.

The panic of 1907 ended on November 7 thanks in no small part to the genius and character of only one man who could whip all the presidents of the New York banks and trust companies. It took a strong man with the will and character to be able to stop what would have been the most calamitous financial event in the history of the United States.

Crashes have been averted since that time without Pierpont's presence, and many may point to that as evidence of its ease in rescue. What most do not understand, however, is that Pierpont was a private banker. He did not wield the force of government. In the years that followed, the Federal Reserve Bank took on the role that Pierpont had in the days right after the Crash of 1907.

Chapter 12 The Rise of Morgan

Pierpont was an extremely powerful man by now. He had saved the United States from a financial crisis twice, and he was the most powerful banker on Wall Street. He may not have been very rich if compared with the likes of Carnegie and Rockefeller, although his wealth was quite impressive at the time. The year 1907 was, however, the last time that any banker would wield as much power and would be more powerful and more capable than the government for fixing a crisis in the nation.

After the panic, future President Woodrow Wilson, who was at the time the president of Princeton University, said that the United States should have a group of people to advise it and suggested that Pierpont be its chairman.

Following the panic, Senator Nelson Wilmarth Aldrich said that something needed to be done. His exact words were, "Something has got to be done. We may not always have Pierpont Morgan with us to meet a banking crisis."

The panic of 1907 led to the formation of the Federal Reserve System, which was established on December 23, 1913, just under nine months after Pierpont's passing.

The power that Pierpont wielded and his purchase of the TCI shares from Moore and Schley during the panic of 1907 inspired a lot of investigation into him.

He was so powerful that people didn't believe he amassed that power through honest work, but that he must have had some sort of illegal or illicit activities to gain that much power. People also thought that perhaps Pierpont had used the panic of 1907 to his advantage, which is true. That is how success is achieved. You have to make use of every single opportunity to be successful.

He lost $21 million during the panic, but he did a great deal for the country. If he had not intervened or did not have the power to fix the situation, Wall Street might have collapsed and suffered irreparable damage. The country itself might even have been in serious trouble. He saved Wall Street and the country, but people chose to focus on illicit things he *might* have done and that he was "too" powerful.

The United States Steel Corporation employed blacks and criminals. Thanks to the Black Codes and the laws made by the states in the South after the Reconstruction era, US Steel was able to hire blacks and pay them very little. It was much cheaper to hire blacks in those times than it was to hire the typical white American. Criminals were also employed, and many died from extremely poor working conditions, lack of food, and abuse. Some of them were not even paid at all.

This practice of hiring criminals and blacks did not stop until the latter part of the 1920s. Besides US Steel, eight of the states in the South also followed this practice.

The United States Steel Corporation was best known perhaps for its unprecedented size rather than for the way it was run. In 1901, the trust was dominating the better part of the steel market as well as manufacturing other products. US Steel also built the largest number of passenger ships under the Pittsburgh Steamship Company.

Because US Steel had large debts, Carnegie, who was involved in the trust, wanted to be paid in gold bonds for his part of the company. US Steel was wary of antitrust policies and tread very carefully.

In 1911, ten years after US Steel was founded, its market share of the steel industry dropped to half. That same year a certain James Augustine Farrell Sr. became president of US Steel. Thanks to him, US Steel expanded. He also founded the Isthmian Steamship Company, which helped with exports of the company. It was thanks to him that the company became the first billion dollar corporation. He remained president of US Steel for twenty-one years until 1932.

After having solved the financial panic of 1907, Pierpont was already partially retired, spending more of his time relaxing and enjoying himself. Because of his shrewd ways and great skill in banking, several conservatives extolled him for what he had done, for he had improved the economy and generally contributed to the betterment of the American financial world. Left wing liberals, however, censured and politically attacked Pierpont for how he had handled the gold standard issue back in 1895 and how he had solved the panic of 1907.

In December 1912, Pierpont stood before a subcommittee of the House Banking and Currency Committee (the Pujo Committee) and said something that made the crowd cheer. The man who was posing the questions to Pierpont at the committee, Mr. Samuel Untermyer, asked him, "Is not commercial credit based primarily upon money or property?" Pierpont replied, "No, sir. The first thing is character." Untermyer then asked, "Before money or property?" Pierpont replied with, "Before money or anything else. Money cannot buy it.... Because a man I do not trust could not get money from me on all the bonds in Christendom." Pierpont was able to win back the favor of the public through his reply.

In the end, the Pujo Committee concluded that J.P. Morgan and Company, as well as the National City Bank and the First National Bank, were controlling $22.245 billion worth of material. After all, Pierpont's bank was controlling the largest steel producer ever in the United States that was dominating the production of all kinds of products, from nails to ships. The $22.245 billion that Pierpont and his associate banks dealt with would later be compared to the wealth of all the states west of the Mississippi River.

During the investigations, it was also found that partners of J.P. Morgan and Company were directors on the boards of 112 different companies, with a total capitalization of more than $22 billion, which was not much less than the capitalization of the New York Stock Exchange at the time, which had more than $26 billion.

Pierpont was now partially retired by the time he had solved the financial panic of 1907, and he spent more of his time relaxing and winding down in his last few years. Sadly, however, he would not have many years left.

The Financial Reserve System was born after the panic of 1907. A financial panic was taking place on average every ten years, and the American government needed a system to cushion the effects of a panic. The Federal Reserve System was meant to act as an organization that would provide money to borrowers in the country for the worst possible cases during a financial panic. The creation of the Federal Reserve Act would lead to the formation of the Federal Reserve System.

After the panic, Roosevelt wanted the government to control the different stock exchanges in the country. Charles Evans Hughes, who was a governor from New York, wished for interest rates on margin loans to be increased to 20 percent. The original interest rate was 10 percent.

In 1908, the Aldrich-Vreeland Currency Act was passed, which led to the creation of the National Monetary Commission to understand the way banks functioned and worked in the United States as well as European countries. After the creation of the National Monetary Commission, Pierpont tried to lead his firm to have a hold on the organization.

Senator Nelson Wilmarth Aldrich was chairman of the National Monetary Commission.

Henry Pomeroy Davison was the only banker who was in Aldrich's sphere. He would be the agent of bankers and stand for their values. George W. Perkins wrote a telegram saying, "It is understood that Davison is to represent our views and will be particularly close to Senator Aldrich."

Mr. Davison had worked alongside Pierpont during the 1907 panic, and before leaving with Aldrich and his associates for Europe to see the central banks of the Continent, he went to meet with Pierpont.

Pierpont was hoping there would be a central bank of the U.S. government that was private and similar to the Bank of England.

Not all politicians liked the idea of a central bank. Such people as the Populists and William Jennings Bryan thought that perhaps a central bank would be run by the bankers of Wall Street, people that both Bryan and the Populists despised. They also saw a central bank as an organization that would bring an end to a group of people known as the Silverites. These people believed that silver should be part of the money system in the United States in the same way as gold.

Pierpont did not mind a central bank as long as it was a private organization and that bankers were its directors. Henry Davison was the "representative" of all bankers and of Pierpont Morgan and was able to advocate the needs of bankers. He, too, thought that a central bank should be run not by politicians but by bankers.

In November 1910, several bankers from Wall Street and Davison met on Jekyll Island, where their meeting was very hush-hush indeed. They formed the Jekyll Island Club.

Jekyll Island was a place Pierpont went when he wanted to separate himself from the whirlwind Republic of America and decompress.

On Jekyll Island, the bankers met and discussed the foundations of a central bank. They talked about how banks in different areas of the country would be established and would be headed by bankers on a board.

Mr. Davison was the man who orchestrated these meetings.

In 1910, Senator N.W. Aldrich approached Congress with a bill for a central bank, but it was blocked by the Democrats. Three years later, in 1913, Carter Glass, a member of the United States Congress and a Democratic politician from Virginia, created the Federal Reserve Act based on the bill that Aldrich had proposed three years earlier, but he changed quite a lot from what Aldrich had proposed.

After President Woodrow Wilson took office, he wanted a network of a dozen banks established in different areas, with its board of directors filled with people he chose as well as the Treasury Secretary.

At the time, Progressives of the era wished that the central bank of the U.S. government would help curb the immense power of Pierpont's firm. In fact, the exact opposite happened. Pierpont's firm would be able to use the Federal Reserve

System to its advantage and grow ever more powerful, although Pierpont would not be the one to do this.

J.P. Morgan and Company was able to benefit from the Federal Reserve System, for it would be approached by several central banks from different countries all over the world.

In 1909, Roosevelt's time in the White House came to an end, and President William Howard Taft took office. Perkins believed that Taft would support Pierpont's expanding business. After receiving a copy of Taft's inaugural address, he wrote to Pierpont, saying that it was "in all respects conciliatory and harmonizing in tone."

Perkins believed that Taft would not be so difficult with antitrust policies and go after Pierpont's trusts and other trust corporations. He was deeply mistaken. While Pierpont was vacationing in Egypt, Perkins sent him coded telegrams with updates on the new president's staff. He made it seem as if he was the one who chose his staff. One of his telegrams to Pierpont informed him that Franklin MacVeagh had become Treasury Secretary, and that he was the one who recommended him. He went on to say that George Woodward Wickersham would be the Attorney General and finished by saying that the remaining positions were filled in favor of Pierpont's firm.

Perkins was deeply mistaken in his judgment that Taft would be more friendly to Pierpont's firm. Through the entire four years that Taft was president, he would work with and against Pierpont. Taft's fight against Pierpont was even more riled up than Roosevelt's. Two years after Taft became president, he attacked International Harvester and the United States Steel Corporation with antitrust lawsuits.

International Harvester was established in 1902 after the merging of the Deering Harvester Company and McCormick Harvesting Machine Company. The merger was conducted by Pierpont's firm. International Harvester was a concern that manufactured construction machinery, cars, trucks, household items, and agricultural machines. This trust was not greatly disliked by people, for it was actually helping them.

Aside from just going after Pierpont, he also attacked John D. Rockefeller, calling for the breaking up of Standard Oil. Taft also broke up the trust of American Tobacco owned by James Buchanan Duke.

Although the American government was going after large businesses and Pierpont's firm, something else was in play. In the United States, Pierpont's firm was being attacked by the government, but outside the country, the government was working with Pierpont's firm to spread its influence and domination over other countries.

In the past, U.S. bankers and the American government never could get along. Now, however, the world of finance was uniting with the world of politics, and the two forces were working together and mutually benefiting.

In time, the firm of J.P. Morgan and Company would become deeply connected with the American government.

The American government wanted to team up with Pierpont because it wanted to have other countries allow U.S. products in their country. The government also saw it as a way to boost the good of the United States and build its reputation.

As for people like Pierpont, it was a good way to be paid back for their loans. They had the power of the army and the police to get them their money back. When Jacob Schiff, the head of Kuhn, Loeb, and Company, was once thinking about giving a loan to the Dominican Republic, he asked his colleague, "If they do not pay, who will collect these customs duties?" In response, his colleague, Sir Ernest Cassel, said, "Your marines and ours."

The Dominican Republic was going to use the import tax they made to pay back the loan.

During Taft's first year as president, he teamed up with Pierpont to spread American financial dominance in Honduras. Taft also wanted to settle the financial issues of British people who had loaned money based on bonds.

Pierpont's firm was to purchase Honduran bonds, which had existed for some time. In

London, these bonds were being sold very cheaply. After that was done, Philander C. Knox, the Secretary of State, was supposed to place a lien from the United States on the taxes earned by Honduras. Knox was then supposed to sell recently issued bonds of Honduras with the help of Pierpont's firm.

The U.S. Army was to stand behind the plan, but Pierpont did not willingly support it. His firm had been forced by the government to help the government. It was the kind of house that dealt only with certain governments and not low-level, Third World countries, such as Honduras. So, they were not so keen on doing business with it.

Pierpont's son, Jack, once sent a telegram to J.S. Morgan and Company in London, saying, "Negotiations only undertaken because US Government anxious get Honduras settled." This showed that Pierpont's firm actually had no interest in this but was doing it just to get it over with.

Jack and Henry Pomeroy Davison, the banker who was with Aldrich, were not willing to go on with the plan unless they had a contract that guaranteed the bonds. In the end, the American government decided not to follow through with the plan, and that was the end of it.

The place where the new relationship between banker and government was truly exhibited was in China. Again, Pierpont's firm was not interested in a country like China. It was not as organized as the places in which Pierpont's firm operated. The Chinese government was said to have been dishonest, cheating their debtors. Because of conditions in China, most bankers did not like doing business with it, and the firms of Wall Street turned to Japan, China's long-time nemesis.

In China, there were the domains of the British, French, and Germans. Now the Americans wanted a slice of the cake. The British, French, and Germans had established themselves in China when the country did not have enough money to construct railways. Under McKinley's administration, in 1899, John Hay, Secretary of State, established the Open Door policy, a policy that allowed all countries to trade and conduct business with China, but that changed when Taft came into office.

He would try to get the United States an equal share of power that the British, Germans, and French were enjoying in China.

In 1909, the U.S. Department of State forced all the banking firms of Wall Street to begin dealing with China. A group of German, British, and French banking houses were just about ready to lend $25 million to China to construct a railway running from Canton to Shanghai. The railway was called the Hukuang Railway. The Americans then came in and wanted to receive the same percentage of interest that the other banks that loaned money to the Chinese were receiving.

A group of banks comprising the National City Bank, Kuhn, Loeb and Company, and the First National Bank was called the American Bankers Group. It was headed by Pierpont's firm according to the wishes of the Department of State.

Before this, these banks fought each other during the cornering of the Northern Pacific

Railroad, and now they were being brought together by the American government, which believed that if these banks worked together American dominance would become stronger in other countries.

This group of bankers held their meetings at Pierpont's office on Wall Street. The bankers were being controlled by the State Department, and the government's conduit was Henry Pomeroy Davison. He once told Teddy Grenfell, a partner of J.S. Morgan and Company, "Think it would be very wise if you would casually but firmly point out to those with whom you come in contact that this is a proposition of the Government and not of the Bankers."

At this time, people believed that the U.S. government had the bankers by the neck, and that they were fleeing. As this notion was percolating in the minds of the public, Mr. Henry Davison was saying, "Continue to be governed entirely by wishes of the State Department." In the past, bankers had stood fast and stayed separate from the government, and they were now extremely furious with Davison.

So far, the United States had been trying to bring down the large trusts of the company and suppress the large banks of the financial world, such as J.P. Morgan and Company. What people didn't know was that the American government and the firm they were trying to "suppress" were secretly working together to increase the power of the United States.

Teddy Grenfell was the envoy between the Americans and the French, German, and British banks. He was and would continue to be a bridge between Pierpont's office at 23 Wall Street and the British government.

At this time, the Morgan firms in London and New York were acting in favor of their own governments, which caused a rift between them. Eventually, J.P. Morgan and Company would be an entirely American bank, and everything else was just connected to it.

During Taft's administration, the group of bankers known as the American Bankers Group was how Pierpont conducted business with China. The man who acted as the American

Bankers Group in China was a certain Willard Dickerman Straight.

After graduating from Cornell University, Straight had a job in the Imperial Maritime Customs Service. He worked in Peking and learned to speak Mandarin while he was there. In 1904, during the Russo-Japanese War, he was a reporter for the Associated Press and Reuters to cover the war. During the time Straight was in Seoul when Korea was still one country, he met Edward Henry Harriman, head of the Union Pacific Railroad.

Harriman hired Straight, and his job was to get Harriman a chance to build a much needed Chinese railway.

Roosevelt made Straight general of the U.S. consul in Mukden, a railway hub in Manchuria.

Straight was a very relaxed government official. He played the guitar, sang Kiplingesque, painted in watercolor, and enjoyed life. He said that China was "the storm center of world politics, where everyone more or less is spying on everyone else."

In 1909, Straight met a woman by the name of Dorothy Whitney. She was the daughter of William C. Whitney, who was once a navy secretary. Mr. Whitney had earned lots of money by working in the business of cars, tobacco, and other products. He was also involved with the stock market, buying and selling shares. Both of Dorothy's parents had passed away when she was young, and she was raised by Robert Bacon and his wife, Martha Cowdin.

Dorothy was very much like Straight, and they were engaged two years after they met.

The same year that Straight met Dorothy he became the envy of the American Bankers Group.

In 1910, he worked in Pierpont's headquarters at 23 Wall Street, something he thought was good luck, for the number of the street was the same number as Dorothy's birthday—the date of the month perhaps.

He was quite shocked by how Pierpont's firm controlled the Department of State.

Pierpont once told Pomeroy Davison, "You might as well make it clear that when we want to discuss things with the US Government we want the Secretary of State and not the assistant secretary." Straight once remarked, "It was not difficult to see where the real power lies in this country." These two anecdotes show that Pierpont's firm had more dominance over the American government than the American government had control of *it*.

In the end, whenever the Secretary of State, Philander C. Knox, wanted to meet with the American Bankers Group, he would come to 23 Wall Street.

In 1910, another loan was given to China, which would receive $50 million to reorganize its currency. Straight was very happy about it.

The loan was agreed to the following year by envoys from France, Britain, and Germany as well as by Straight and Chinese government officials. It was at this time that Straight wrote to Dorothy and said, "We've arranged it so that we can practically dictate the terms of China's currency reform. When you think of holding the whip hand in formulating the first real sound financial basis for a country of 400 million, it's quite a proposition."

When everyone found out about the loan, Straight became popular. Aside from the fact that he was connected with Pierpont's behemoth of a firm, he had also been a success regarding the loan to China. Because of this, he gained better favor with Dorothy's parents.

Dorothy's foster father, Robert Bacon, had obviously been acquainted with Pierpont, and Dorothy, being part of his family, was too. She wrote a letter to Straight saying, "Dear Mr. J.P. he's such a sweetie underneath the sternness."

Straight remained at Pierpont's firm for as long as he did perhaps because he liked the benefits he received by simply being connected and being part of the firm.

Straight was overconfident regarding the success of the second loan to China. Both he and other financiers had invested their money in the Manchu government, a corrupt leadership. How was that supposed to work?

The lenders who had loaned their money to the Chinese were going to suffer a loss. Straight wanted to do things in such a way that would prevent the loan from being a failure. What Straight didn't understand was that the Chinese people did not like outside financiers.

In 1912, a conference was held in Paris at which both Russia and Japan wanted to be part of the group that was dealing with China. They were granted their seats.

This was what Straight feared most. He did not at all like the prospect of having China's enemies among the group of bankers that were conducting business with the country.

Straight predicted ". . . the inevitable day when China's finances will be administered like Egypt's—by an international board. Another dream shattered!"

Perhaps this meant that he had been expecting that the Americans would be able to have a dominating effect on China, but his hopes obviously did not materialize.

In 1911, a revolution took place in China. The cause of the revolution was partially because the people did not like overseas bankers meddling with their country. Dorothy, now Straight's wife, supported those who were revolting.

In January 1912, a new China was formed and headed by Sun Yat-sen. He led a group of people to bring China together and push out all outside elements.

During the revolution, Straight kept a loaded revolver next to him. His wife, however, was not at all worried and even thought it would be fun. She wrote, "It would be rather exciting to be attacked by a wild mob in the night."

Willard and Dorothy were once preparing to go out and have dinner with one of their neighbors of British nationality. While they were still in their home, they heard gunshots. Straight described what happened. When the gunshots were heard, he told his wife that perhaps something was wrong. Dorothy wasn't at all bothered and went on preparing herself to meet their neighbor. She was quite undisturbed, and when Straight told her to just wear casual clothing so that if they needed to they could make their way to the Legation, she adamantly refused.

When the gunshots ceased for some time and things were calm for a moment, Straight and his wife headed to the home of their neighbor. Soon, however, soldiers began to rob some shops that were in the vicinity. Straight and his wife then took their housekeeper, some clothes, and headed for the Legation. Unfortunately for them, they ran straight into rioters on a street that was a dead end.

Not very long afterward, a group of American marines freed them. In the end, Straight and his wife were able to make it to the Legation.

After Woodrow Wilson became President of the United States in 1913, America would soon back out of China. William Jennings Bryan, the man who was the greatest threat to Pierpont and all the other titans of industry or finance in America, became Secretary of State under Wilson.

Six days after Wilson took office on March 10, 1913, Straight and Pomeroy Davison came to Washington to meet with Bryan, who was certainly not going to go to 23 Wall Street, the office of one of the people he would have tried to destroy had he become president in 1896. So, 23 Wall Street had to go to him.

At their meeting, Bryan asked what they would want from the American government if the Chinese did not pay their debt. Davison said the American government could "be called upon to utilize both its military and naval forces to protect the interests of the lenders."

What he was basically saying was that if China did not pay its debt he and the American Bankers Group would want military force to get their money back.

Both President Wilson and Bryan were opposed to becoming involved with foreign countries as the previous administration of Taft and bankers of American Bankers Group had been. A week after the meeting Bryan had with Pomeroy and Straight President Wilson said that the loan was "obnoxious to the principles upon which the government of our people rests."

The American Bankers Group was disassembled the next day. It had been a conduit through which the administration was acting, and if the current president did not want it or supported it, it could not exist.

Most bankers were happy that things had happened the way they did, for they were not so sure whether or not China was going to pay its debt. Pierpont's firm was also glad to be done with China.

After everything was over, Teddy Grenfell of J.S. Morgan and Company, who was always working during the China issue, wrote a letter to Jack that read, "I think that all of us will have 'China' written on our hearts when we die, with several uncomplimentary epithets after it."

Although the business with China was a failure and an operation that fell flat on its face, it was a success in another area. It made different banks feel more comfortable about working together in a foreign domain. Such firms as the First

National Bank, J.P. Morgan and Company, and the National City Bank all joined in a specific part of the financing, which biographer Ron Chernow has called in his book about the Morgan house "Latin Lending."

The unification of these three firms caused the already immense power of Pierpont's firm to increase substantially. Several times the firm of Kuhn, Loeb, and Company would join the group of J.P. Morgan and Company, First National Bank, and National City Bank. These would be the banks that would be dubbed the "Money Trust." They would be brought to the Pujo Committee, where Pierpont had testified.

What the American people didn't know was that what they called the "Money Trust" had inadvertently created the "trust" while it was seeking to extend its domain.

The world was entering a time when bankers and governments were one and no longer arch enemies. The effect was so great that a man like Jack, who, like his father, greatly despised the government, was able to pull himself back from being so open about it. In 1912, Jack sent a telegram to Teddy Grenfell, saying, "You will understand we do not wish to accuse our own Government too loudly in view of necessary relations with the other foreign matters."

Although Jack was as headstrong as Pierpont regarding his dislike for the American government, he understood that he could not voice this dislike.

After everything was over, Straight continued to work at the 23 Wall Street office, but he never did feel comfortable working in that slow environment.

When former president Theodore Roosevelt ran again against Taft and Wilson in 1912, he was supported by Straight and his wife.

In 1914, Straight financed *The New Republic*, a weekly magazine/newspaper that strongly supported Theodore Roosevelt when it was first created.

Straight was the kind of man who could not take a slow environment for very long and found working in Pierpont's bank to be quite difficult.

Straight founded the India House, an institution that dealt in trading with other countries. The India House was located in Hanover Square in New York. Straight would continue to work at the Morgan bank for just two more years.

Although a financial genius and a great banker, Pierpont did sometimes choose the wrong ventures to invest in, and they all backfired on him. One such case involved the London Underground. A man by the name of Charles Tyson Yerkes was able to prevent Pierpont from receiving permission from Parliament to build the Piccadilly, City, and North East London Railway. This underground railroad would have been a competitor of Yerkes' railway, the Tube.

Nikola Tesla

Another one of Pierpont's unfortunate business ventures concerned Thomas Alva Edison's rival inventor, Nikola Tesla.

In 1900, Nikola Tesla gained Pierpont's confidence that he would be capable of constructing a wireless communication system that could span the Atlantic Ocean. Pierpont was confident enough to lend Mr. Tesla $150,000, which now would be equivalent to $4,517,400. It was planned that Pierpont would receive control of 51 percent of the patents. After everything was settled, Tesla wanted to quickly expand his venture by constructing a wireless power transmission system that would work on the land. In the end, Pierpont did not want to lend him any more money to do this and did not want anything different from what had been originally discussed. All the money invested was now gone. Tesla's transatlantic communication system was thrown into the dustbin, and that was the end of it.

Chapter 13 The Sun Sets

Pierpont was a sad and lonely man in his last few years. He traveled everywhere and spent a lot of time in Europe and the continent. Before going somewhere, Pierpont would tell Jack where he was going. Pierpont was once asked what his favorite places were. Pierpont said, "New York because it is my home; London because it is my second home; Rome, and Khargeh."

More than any other place, Pierpont greatly loved Egypt. Between 1910 and 1913, he would go to Egypt three times, and he financed the dig sites in Egypt that were being conducted by the Metropolitan Museum.

Just four hundred miles away from Cairo, excavations were taking place at the oasis of Khargeh. He was deeply interested in the excavations and asked the ship-building concern of Thomas Cook and Son that a ship meant to sail on the Nile River be called the *Khargeh*.

Pierpont would later stand on the *Khargeh* and throw coins into the Nile. Children would jump into the river and fetch them.

But Pierpont was a lonely man, and one of his biographers wrote, "It is said there are scarcely fifty men in the financial district who have a speaking acquaintance with Morgan." Only a few people were really close to him. His family provided him at least a little happiness.

What would be especially painful for him occurred when his daughter would be ripped away from him after having been convinced that she was being used by her father by a certain Bessie Marbury.

This daughter of Pierpont's was the philanthropist Anne Tracy Morgan. She was a mischievous child and took after her father in several ways. She was a jolly, active young child, who liked to play tennis and golf. She was also very difficult to handle when raising her to be a member of the aristocracy.

Anne was smart, authoritative, always had her view of things, and headstrong like her father. A certain Elizabeth Drexel, who would go on to become the wife of Harry Lehr, said that Anne was "a thin lanky child with an elfin face and penetrating eyes." Miss Drexel also described her as a child with "a personality and a will as strong as Pierpont's own and a disconcerting habit of putting her elders in the wrong."

Anne would sometimes insultingly mock her father. One time when Pierpont was having dinner with some of his colleagues he asked Anne what she wanted to be when she grew older. She said, "Something better than a rich fool, anyway." Although she would mock and insult him, she was also close to him and would go with Pierpont on *Corsair III* when he was going to Europe.

When the Kaiser of Germany was once on board her father's yacht, she was the one who tended to him.

At the beginning of the twentieth century, Anne had become a woman who was much like her father. She possessed Pierpont's chilling stare and absolutely despised the drawings that exaggerated and insulted Pierpont because of his nose. She also despised the people who drew them.

Pierpont was a man that liked high-quality and beautiful clothing. His daughter also liked fine clothing.

In 1903, a lady from Washington by the name of Daisy Harriman got Anne to be a cofounder of the first ladies club in the United States, the Colony Club. It was located on 30th Street and Madison Avenue and was made to look like a British club that was for men. It had several Turkish baths and a swimming pool made of marble.

One of the rules of the club was that all men who visited were not allowed to go above the first floor. Pierpont did not like the club and said, "A woman's best and safest club is her own home."

During the time in which the Colony Club was coming into existence, Anne met Elsie de Wolfe and Bessie Marbury. Wolfe was once an actress and quite well-known. She furnished the Colony Club.

In 1901, Anne, Wolfe, and Marbury began to live together in Villa Trianon in Versailles.

For several years, Anne and her two colleagues would create many pro-feminine institutions and achieve a great many things. One of these was creating a dance hall for Broadway and bankrolling the first musical of American composer and songwriter Cole Albert Porter.

When some female workers once went on strike, Anne supported them. She also started a temperance restaurant in Brooklyn and founded an organization as a fund to provide for young and employed women to take a holiday.

In 1908, Anne had lunch with President Roosevelt in the White House, and Roosevelt was only too happy to be thinking about the uncomfortable state of Pierpont.

Pierpont did not at all like his daughter's behavior. She really was very different from the rest of society.

Certain people who attended the parties and events of Anne and her colleagues included

Maxine Elliott and Bernard Berenson. Elliott was once one of Pierpont's mistresses.

Like her father, Anne was always smoking and also very popular. After all, she was ranked among the wealthiest young women in the world. Aristocratic Europeans constantly approached her.

False information once got out that she was engaged to marry a count from France by the name of Boni de Castellane.

At one point, the relationship between Anne and Pierpont would sour thanks to Bessie Marbury. Bessie told Anne that she was being used by her father to cover up his extramarital affairs, and that was why he taken her on his yacht. This was what made Anne separate from her father. One other possible cause is that when she found out about the affairs themselves she was greatly upset about them.

Anne's siblings did not look favorably upon her attitude toward her father.

The breaking of the relationship between Pierpont and his daughter was very painful for him and unimaginably saddening. A friend of Anne's said, "It broke her father's heart when she elected to part from him."

In the end, Pierpont would get his revenge on Bessie Marbury.

Bessie Marbury deeply wanted to be awarded the French Legion of Honor. During her career, she had spoken on behalf of playwrights from France. She had also volunteered her house in Versailles as a hospital during the First World War. She had also been able to put together money for the country. This was obviously after Pierpont's passing because he died in March 1913.

This is where Pierpont would get his revenge. He would stop her from winning that award. In 1909, Robert Bacon became the American ambassador to France. Pierpont did not want Marbury to get the award, and Bacon honored his wishes.

When the French were informed that Pierpont did not support the idea of Marbury receiving the award, France did not want to give it to her.

Although past presidents of the United States, such as William Howard Taft and Theodore Roosevelt, supported Marbury, the French were not going to give it to her at the cost of going against J.P. Morgan.

During the last few years of Pierpont's life, his relationship with Jack strengthened and was quite good. Although Jack provided emotional backing for his father, there were a few things he vowed never to do, such as have extramarital affairs. He remained faithful and loyal to his wife, Jessie. Due to Jack's innate low self-confidence and lack of ambition, he would not be as great as Pierpont while heading the Morgan house. He would run it well but not as powerful and impactful as his father.

In 1910, he fell to the ground from extreme exhaustion. Because of his feelings that he was not good enough and could not handle everything, after the incident, he wanted someone else to generally run things. Jack took a more overall position and led the bank as a whole.

In the end, Jack became the leader of the Morgan house, but two other people wanted to be the leader: George W. Perkins and Henry Pomeroy Davison. There were several problems with having Perkins as the leader of the Morgan bank. On one hand, problems had arisen with him when he worked at the New York Life Insurance Company.

In his mind, he also placed himself at the top and forgot that he *served* the firm.

Perkins owned a home and land around it in Riverdale. His home was furnished with a bowling alley, swimming pool, and ballroom. He also had nine servants. Finally, he owned a custom-made car. It was eleven feet long and furnished with a washstand table as well as a desk.

He was very haughty regarding the Morgan bank. He thought that he was better qualified that Pierpont's son to be the next leader of the House of Morgan.

Sometimes, he would do things without first discussing them with the firm. In 1910, for example, Pomeroy Davison and Pierpont had a conversation in which Pierpont said that Perkins had gone against what he wanted regarding the financing agreement of the Studebaker Company. Pomeroy then told Perkins about what Pierpont said, and Perkins then sent a letter to Pierpont, which read, "I am very deeply disturbed by one remark that Davison made, viz., that you felt I had gone ahead and deliberately disregarded an understanding with you and concluded the business to suit myself."

George W. Perkins would leave the House of Morgan in six months. He was kicked out of the bank. Thomas William Lamont Jr. recounted that Perkins "didn't leave on his own accord. Morgan thought he had been a little second-rate on some deals."

Regarding Henry Pomeroy Davison, he was on the path to becoming the chief operating executive of J.P. Morgan and Company.

Davison was from a not very well-to-do family. His father sold farming equipment, and he and his family were quite poor. When Henry applied to Harvard University with a scholarship application, he was rejected. He did not go to school.

One of his early jobs was working in a bank that was in Bridgeport, Connecticut, the state in which Pierpont Morgan was born. One of the directors of the bank, a certain P.T. Barnum, liked Davison and asked him to come and play whist with him every week.

In 1893, Pomeroy married Miss Kate Trubee. He and his newly wedded wife then moved to New York. There, Davison worked in the Astor Trust Company. During his time there, a robbery occurred, which he handled well.

The robber stood before the window in front of Davison at his desk and pointed a gun at him. The robber then gave a check for $1 million and told him to give him the money that was stated on the check. Davison began to count out the money in small notes.

As Davison was going about his business deliberately slowly, the guard of the bank was able to get the police on the scene, and they arrested the robber when they arrived.

At a later date, Baker would come to him and say, "Davison, I think you'd better move your desk up here with us." Davison became the vice president of the First National Bank. He also assisted in founding Bankers Trust.

During the panic of 1907, Davison was involved in talks and discussions regarding the panic and later acted on behalf of the financial hub that was Wall Street on the National Monetary Commission. He soon caught Pierpont's attention.

Stories about Davison show that he was a man who was joyful, confident, and hardworking.

He also enjoyed hunting and killed such animals as elephants, rhinoceroses, moose, antelope, and hippopotamuses.

He also liked to spend time with others and talk to people. He would hold dinners at his Peacock Point home, where he often had at least twenty guests.

When Davison joined Pierpont's bank, he brought with him several skilled people, including Ben Strong, Thomas Lamont, John Davis, and Dwight Morrow.

Thomas Lamont was the most valuable person that Davison brought to Pierpont's firm.

After Lamont left college, he became a reporter for the *New York Tribune* while studying at Harvard University. He later quit being a reporter and went to work at Cushman Bros., which was a company that advertised different companies in the food industry. It was not doing very well financially, and Lamont was able to save the company, and after doing so their name was rechristened Lamont, Corliss, and Company. He basically became a partner.

Soon, Lamont became known for helping out Wall Street concerns, which attracted Davison's attention.

Lamont was the kind of person who did not have to crawl through the mud and trenches to get what he wanted. He could easily sail through and be successful.

In 1903, Lamont, who was now thirty-three years old, was on a train heading for Englewood.

This is when he met Henry Pomeroy Davison. When Lamont got onto the train, Davison was thinking about who would be the treasury secretary at Bankers Trust. Davison would approach Lamont about the position.

Lamont replied, "But I don't know the first thing about banking. All my brief business life I have been borrowing money—not lending it." Davison then said, "Fine, that's just why we want you. A fearless borrower like you ought to make a prudent lender." Lamont took the job and later became vice president of Bankers Trust. He would eventually become a director.

Six years after taking the job as treasury secretary he would become the vice president of the First National Bank. A year later he would be called to the Morgan bank by Pierpont himself.

When they met, Pierpont told him, "You see that room over there? It's vacant." He went on to say, "Beginning next Monday, I want you to occupy it." Lamont acted completely surprised. He then said, "But what can I do for you that is worthwhile?" His answer was, "Oh, you'll find plenty to keep you busy. Just do whatever you see before you that needs to be done."

Lamont was not entirely "game on" about the proposal though. He once spoke with Pierpont and told him that he wanted to travel for three months at a time on an annual basis. Pierpont was not at all irritated or angered and said, "Why, of course, take off as much time as you like. That is entirely in your hands."

Lamont was actually very skilled and could handle situations very well, but he acted very humble, and that just made him more liked.

In his last few years, Pierpont made it clear what was to happen to J.S Morgan and Co. When Pierpont's father was alive, he said that the firm of J.S. Morgan and Co. should exist for as long as one generation or as long as Pierpont's lifetime. Thus, he made it so that his name could be used. Twenty years had nearly passed since Junius' passing in 1890, and Jack said, "As we approached 1910, father said, 'You will have trouble enough when I die without having to think of a new name for this firm, and I suggest that we should now change it to Morgan,

Grenfell & Co. and make J.P. Morgan & Co. partners in it. They do keep one million pounds in capital."

On January 1, 1910, J.S. Morgan and Company was renamed Morgan, Grenfell, and Company. This was the first time ever that the House of Morgan had a British name as part of a name of one its representatives or in the name of any firm of the House of Morgan.

Jack and his father were previously partners of J.S. Morgan and Co. Now, the entire firm of J.P. Morgan and Co. was a partner of Morgan, Grenfell, and Company. The direct firm under Pierpont would take 50 percent of the profits made by the London firm.

The way that Pierpont had structured his banking empire was that his office at 23 Wall Street was the center of it all—the capital of the Morgan Empire.

Atlantic Transport

Bernard Nadal Baker owned the Atlantic Transport Line, which owned both passenger ships and cargo ships. He once attempted to sell the Atlantic Transport Line to a certain John Ellerman, who was the chairman of the board of directors for the Leyland Line, a purely cargo ship company. Talks were held, but Ellerman did not purchase Baker's company.

Ellerman had also attempted to take control of the HAPAG shipping company and the Cunard Line.

It was at this time that Pierpont finished finalizing things with the International Navigation Company's president, Clement Griscom. The International Navigation Company controlled both the American Line and the Red Star Line. After talks that lasted for six months, the International Navigation Company merged with the Atlantic Transport Line in December 1900.

Two more companies would soon join the corporation that would be the IMMC: the White Star Line and the Leyland Line, a company where Ellerman was a director. Finally, the International Mercantile Marine Company was established on October 1, 1902.

Pierpont's last year was stressful and painful for him. On one side, the International Mercantile Marine Company was dealing with fierce competition from the Cunard Line, and a disaster would take place that would drive him into a state of grief.

Titanic

The Cunard Line had by now constructed the RMS Lusitania and the RMS Mauretania.

To contend with their major competitor, the IMMC decided to build two new gargantuan ships—the RMS Olympic and the RMS Titanic, both of which belonged to the White Star Line. To have enough room for these ships, Pierpont's firm tried to get the New York Harbor Board to make one of the piers of the Hudson River longer by one hundred feet so that the Titanic and the Olympic could dock at it.

The RMS Titanic was launched on May 31, 1911. Pierpont was present for the launch. He climbed aboard the ship, where he saw the cabin made for him to travel on during the ship's maiden voyage. It was wonderfully furnished, and the bathroom had a special container for his enormous cigars.

Pierpont was supposed to travel on the first trip of the Titanic but cancelled at the last minute. Just think about it: J.P. Morgan was about to go on the ship that would sink to the bottom of the Atlantic Ocean.

On April 16, 1912, the day after the RMS Titanic sank, Pierpont learned of the catastrophe while he was in France. He sent a telegram to an associate of his in New York saying, "Have just heard a fearful rumor about Titanic with the iceberg." He went on to say, "Without any particulars. Hope for God sake not true."

After everyone knew of the calamity, the press of the continent found Pierpont at a chateau. He looked absolutely saddened and depressed. At one time, he said, "Think of the lives that have been mowed down and of the terrible deaths." The sinking of the Titanic greatly affected him. Not only had his firm invested in the company that built the ship, but a great many people had also died.

Of the more than two thousand people who sailed on the Titanic, more than one thousand five hundred died in the accident. Some went down with the ship, and others jumped into the ocean but tired out from the bitter cold and drowned too.

Those that survived the disaster were rescued by the Carpathia, a ship belonging to the Cunard Line.

The sinking of the Titanic caused a serious financial problem for the IMMC. The situation became so severe that in 1915 the company had to seek protection from bankruptcy, which limited the amount of money it could spend to settle its debts. At the time, the IMMC was doing so poorly that it did not have enough money to pay their interest on bonds. At the end of the First World War, the IMMC became known as the United States Lines, a company that would last until 1986, when it would go bankrupt.

Yachts

The first yacht that Pierpont owned was the *Corsair*. It was actually built for a man by the name of Charles J. Osborn by the William Cramp and Sons company. It was ready by May 26, 1880, and Pierpont purchased it two years later.

Pierpont eventually got a second yacht, the *Corsair II*. Sadly for Pierpont, the U.S. Navy included this yacht in its fight against the Spanish in the Spanish-American War. The navy paid Pierpont $225,000 and in 1898 turned it into the gunboat *USS Gloucester*. It fought at the Battle of Santiago, where it was hit by an enemy shell. A fragment of the mast was kept by Pierpont, who was not even willing to give up the ship in the first place.

Feeling so passionate about the loss of his yacht, Pierpont built another yacht, *Corsair III*. This third yacht was really quite regal.

When Pierpont traveled on passenger ships, upon his return he would stand on the deck and wave his handkerchief. His yacht would pull up to collect him, and he would simply disembark from the cruise ship and board his own. This way he did not have to go through quarantine.

Voyages always seemed to be the best cure for Pierpont regardless of how he felt. When he fell into his usual depressions, nothing but a trip at sea would cheer him up.

Pierpont would spend nights on the *Corsair*, and at the beginning of the weekend, he would take some friends with him to his Cragston home. On Sunday evening, they would travel back on the yacht to Manhattan and spend the night on the yacht. The following morning they would enjoy a splendid breakfast, leave the ship, and go off to their respective businesses.

Sea trips were the only thing that made Pierpont happy. Even his successes and his accomplishments did not make him joyful or proud. In fact, they made him more depressed. Jack, wrote to his mother, saying, "JPM has been so worried and bothered by the number of things on his mind and this annoyance of war rumor that it will be a great thing for him to have this voyage. Then if things calm down … he will come back for his Aix cure and get two more voyages. Those are the only things which really seem to do him any good."

It's possible that this letter Jack wrote to his mother was because he was trying to protect her from knowing that her husband had been participating in extramarital affairs, but Pierpont was happiest at sea.

In response to Pierpont's failing health, his physicians advised him to relax. He obeyed, which is why he bought his yacht. Aboard his boat, he not only conducted business and settled matters but also enjoyed himself.

Pierpont also created the Metropolitan Club. He had previously been a member of the Union Club but left after a friend of his, a man by the name of John King, who was at the time the president of the Erie Railroad, was rejected from joining the club. After the Metropolitan Club was established, King became part of the club, and Pierpont was president of the club from 1891 to 1900.

Pierpont wasn't too excited about having all kinds of land. He did, however, have truly grand homes. The house at 219 Madison Avenue was constructed in 1853 by the publisher John Jay Phelps. Pierpont bought the house in 1882.

This home was also the home in which his daughter Juliet Pierpont married her husband, William Pierson Hamilton. Their wedding took place on April 12, 1894, and a thousand people attended it. As a gift, they were given Pierpont's favorite clock.

Pierpont also owned a summer house on East Island in Glen Cove in Nassau County. That house has recently been priced at $125 million.

Besides being an art collector, Pierpont also collected jewelry. As for his art collecting, he had a vast store that had either been given or loaned to the Metropolitan Museum of Art. In fact, Pierpont was once president of the Metropolitan Museum of Art. Many art pieces were kept in Pierpont's house in London. More were kept in Pierpont's private library not too far from the Empire State Building.

Eventually, his home could not house his many art pieces, which is why he built the Pierpont Morgan Library. It was a place for him to store his collection.

Following Pierpont's will, Jack opened the Pierpont Morgan Library to the public in 1924. The first director of the library was Bella Da Costa Greene. Bella was the caretaker of the library when Pierpont was alive and when it was still a private library. She was probably a mistress of Pierpont, and Pierpont was so jealous of her that when she was having an affair with another man, she told that man to keep their relationship secret so as to not rile Pierpont.

Jack liked her but in a strictly friendly manner.

Several artists painted pictures of Pierpont, including the South American Carlos Baca-Flor, a Peruvian artist, and Adolfo Müller-Ury, who was Swiss but born in the United States. Ury had painted a picture of Pierpont with the son of Juliet Pierpont, Mabel Satterlee, who was Pierpont's favorite grandchild.

This painting was kept on an easel in the mansion of the Satterlee family but has now disappeared.

Gems

As for gem collecting, Pierpont had more than one thousand in his collection. The company that put together Pierpont's first gem collection was Tiffany and Company. The collection was placed under a gemologist by the name of George Frederick Kunz.

Pierpont's gem collection was displayed in 1889 during the World's Fair in Paris. This display received two golden awards. Mr. Kunz built another collection of gems, which was displayed in Paris in 1900. Both of these collections were given to the American Museum of Natural History and were called the Morgan-Tiffany and the Morgan-Bemment collections. Eleven years after the display of Kunz's second collection a new gem discovered by Kunz was named after Pierpont. It was called Morganite.

Pierpont also helped the photographer Edward S. Curtis. In 1906, Pierpont loaned Curtis $75,000 to create a photographic series of Native Americans. In 1907, Mr. Curtis would publish the book *The North American Indian*. In

1914, Curtis sponsored the film *In the Land of the Head Hunters*. In 1974, it was redone and retitled *In the Land of the War Canoes*. Another film was shown three years later. It was called *The Indian Picture Opera*. It was a slideshow shown by a magic lantern. The film included the photographs of Curtis and music composed by Henry F. Gilbert.

After testifying before the Pujo Committee, Pierpont returned to one of his most ardent passions. He traveled.

Unfortunately, however, during his last few months, he would be afflicted with constant health problems. He suffered from panic attacks, digestive problems, insomnia, and depression. Pierpont was so ill that Jack wanted to come and be with him, but Jack's older sister told him, "Your suggestion coming yourself has touched and pleased him, but he is anxious you should remember how much depends upon your being on the spot in New York—how many interests are in your hands. He is too weak to make a decision; he wishes to leave it you." This was the first time in Jack's entire life that Pierpont had entrusted him with that great a responsibility and given him that powerful and meaningful a position. Pierpont basically made his son acting leader of the House of Morgan while he was ill.

Pierpont was very ill and couldn't sleep. He was in so much pain that even morphine did not make him feel better. He was always uncomfortable and unsettled. When he passed away on March 3, he was disoriented and kept thinking back to when he was a boy. He thought of himself being at school and said that his fellow classmates were "a fine lot of boys."

Pierpont had already been feeling ill before he left for Egypt. In Egypt, his illness was compounded by a fever that he contracted there. When he arrived in Rome, physicians tended to him, but his condition worsened. After some time, he was not able to speak and had to communicate with his family that was with him by writing and later only by sign language. Lesions formed on his brain, and his condition grew so bad that by Easter Sunday he became disoriented and went into a state of constant delirium.

He had been able to eat before, and his food was a liquid substance that was given through a tube. He was doing well when he ate but at one point did not want to eat. He began to lose weight rapidly, and his strength plummeted.

Approximately one hour before Pierpont passed away, the doctors who tended to him asked his family to leave the room so that they would be not there to witness his passing, which might have been made ugly by seizures and exhibitions of pain.

The last words of one of the greatest bankers in the history of the world—"I've got to go up the hill." He had already lost his mind and was delerious.

He died shortly after midnight, just over two weeks before his seventy-sixth birthday. Not long afterward, 3,697 people as well as the pope sent telegrams to the Grand Hotel giving their condolences.

Conclusion

It is not an exaggeration to claim that John Pierpont Morgan Sr. was one of the greatest bankers in the world. During the last eighteen years of his life, he accomplished things that most men, rich or poor, could not even dream of. He created the company that was once the biggest steel producer in the United States. He reorganized several railroads and saved the country from two financial crises.

He had amassed so much power and influence that people of lesser minds and even lesser imagination believed he was not honest in his ways. He saved the country, but he was persecuted in return.

He grew his businesses and banks into vast empires, creating one of the largest banks ever to exist. He was a man that although successful went through a lot of pain and heartache. He had lost the love of his life just after he married her. He loved his children, but he felt that his son was not strong enough. His daughter turned against him, and the two of them had been extremely close. She had turned against him because of mistakes he made while he was in pain and unhappy.

He was not only one of the most successful men in the world but also one of the saddest. He had all that power but no happiness—no source of light. He was extremely stressed during his last several years. The sinking of the Titanic was a great pang to his heart, and the investigations led against him and the presidents he had to fight and the anger he had for the top-hat politicians of Washington caused him a lot of pain and stress.

He was a man who worked hard for his success, and he changed the way the world works. He changed the way the financial world operated, and he created a foundation for new systems of banking among the firms of Wall Street, and he invested in things that still benefit the world today.

Aside from what happened in the external world, he was insecure because of his nose and outward appearance. He was so worried about his appearance that he became bitter.

Before he met Amelia Sturges, even when he had a limp, he was still a happy young man. It was only after her death that he became bitter and unhappy. That unhappiness would last for the rest of his life.

After Pierpont's death, the house that Pierpont built was taken over by Jack.

In today's world, J.P. Morgan Sr. would be worth approximately $41.5 billion. He may not have been as rich as the oil magnate John D. Rockefeller or the steel tycoon Andrew Carnegie, but he was rich in a way that couldn't be accounted for in monetary terms. He made a difference in the world. He changed the way the financial world worked. The difference between someone like J.P. Morgan and a banker that just wants to make money is that Pierpont constantly strived for more glory and success. The banker who just wants money will do anything for it. He will cheat, steal, and be corrupt. Pierpont Morgan gained his power through hard work, but many people thought he must have been corrupt.

For Pierpont, he cared about getting what he wanted to be done. As he said, "I don't know as I want a lawyer to tell me what I cannot do. I hire him to tell how to do what I want to do." Pierpont did not like obstacles and problems. He wanted what he wanted, and nothing was going to stop that. His techniques of structuring and reorganizing companies made his firm the largest bank in the world. This was thanks to his ambition and his unrelenting character that strived for even more success despite his feelings that he wanted to retire. The decisions he made before he started his career in banking when he bought the entire shipment of Brazilian coffee to when he solved the 1895 gold standard issue or how he settled the 1907 financial panic shows that he did not care for rules or regulations. All he knew was that there was something he wanted to be done, and he was going to do it regardless of the risks. For instance, he did not care for problems involving antitrusts. He took care of them, but that did not stop him from achieving his goal.

Decades after Pierpont's death the bank he built would grow so powerful that the U.S. government would force it to break down. In 1931, Morgan Stanley was formed. In the 1950s, Morgan Guaranty came into existence. Near the end of 2000, Chase Bank merged with J.P. Morgan and Company and paid $36 billion in bonds. These two firms formed JPMorgan Chase. Aside from just consisting of J.P. Morgan and Co. and Chase Bank, it also includes Washington Mutual, Bank One, and Bear Stearns.

Although J.P. Morgan and Company no longer exists on its own, and its successor is not the largest bank in the world, his firm is still very meaningful. It was created through hard work and careful planning based on mistakes that Pierpont had learned from and taken to heart. Everything that Pierpont got he worked for.

In the end, John Pierpont Morgan Sr. left this world different from how it was when he entered it. He changed the world and left his mark on it.

We—you and I—live in the world crafted by the will of John Pierpont Morgan.

If you enjoyed learning about J.P. Morgan and the founding of the American Banking System, I would be forever grateful if you could leave a review on Amazon. Reviews are the best way for readers to give feedback to newer authors like myself. Thanks in advance!

And make sure to check out the other books in this series!

Printed in Great Britain
by Amazon